The Macintosh
DIC'TION·AR·Y

Written and Illustrated by
Andy Baird

Edited by Sharon Zardetto Aker

THAUMATURGE
BOOKS

Addison-Wesley Publishing Company

Reading, Massachusetts • Menlo Park, California

New York • Don Mills, Ontario • Wokingham, England

Amsterdam • Bonn • Sydney • Singapore • Tokyo • Madrid

San Juan • Paris • Seoul • Milan • Mexico City • Taipei

Library of Congress Cataloging-in-Publication Data

Baird, Andy.
     The Macintosh Dictionary / Andy Baird; edited by Sharon Zardetto Aker.
         p.   cm.
     Includes index.
     ISBN 0-201-60886-3
     1. Macintosh (Computer) I. Aker, Sharon Zardetto. II. Title.
QA76.8.M3B35 1992
004.165--dc20   92-9796
                                                         CIP

Sponsoring Editor: Julie Stillman
Project Editor: Elizabeth Rogalin
Production Coodinator: Kathy Traynor
Technical Editor: Russ Ito
Cover design: Virginia Evans & Rob Day
Text design: Thaumaturge, Inc., and John Luttropp
Set in 9-point Hiroshige by Jerry Szubin for Thaumaturge, Inc.

1 2 3 4 5 6 7 8 9-MU-9695949392
First printing, May 1992

This book is gratefully dedicated to

Gretchen, who inspired it,

and

Sharon, who made it easy.

Contents

Acknowledgments

Like most books, this one owes its existence to many good people. First I want to thank the members of the Princeton Mac Users' Group. Much of what I know about the Mac I learned at PMUG meetings and from fellow PMUG members.

Sharon Aker was the perfect midwife for this, my first book; her knowledge and professionalism saved me from untold trouble and frustration. Thanks are also due to Elizabeth Rogalin and the gang at Addison-Wesley, whose patience with this new author's missteps was equaled by their willingness to try out new production methods. I'm especially grateful to Susan Riley, my copy editor. Her thorough and meticulous checking made this book a much better one than it would have been otherwise, and also taught me a thing or two about tightening up my prose.

Our resident Mac Dictionary composer, Frank Lewin, earned my gratitude by transcribing the Chimes of Doom in musical notation (I believe for the first time anywhere), and Rick Farmer's suggestions on networking jargon added much to this book.

Finally, my undying gratitude goes to the good people at Steelcase office furniture. Without their model 430312 office chair—the most comfortable I've ever owned—this book would surely never have been finished. (And best of all, I got the chair for peanuts at the Trenton Computer Festival flea market!)

—*Andy*

We also want to thank Jerry Szubin for laying out the book several times without complaining about the rewrites (his picture's in the entry for *halftone*); Rich Wolfson, for considered opinions and other odds and ends; and Nicholas and Nathaniel Aker, for using one of their vacation days (from sixth and fourth grades, respectively) to help print, collate, and even proofread the final pages.

—*Sharon*

Introduction

Computer jargon has its uses; it's a shorthand language that can save a lot of unnecessary verbiage. (How fast can you say "Single Inline Memory Module"? Now try "SIMM.") But it's only useful when everybody understands the same shorthand. This dictionary is your guide to the language of computers in general and the Macintosh in particular.

For someone new to the world of the Macintosh, all this unfamiliar vocabulary is probably the single biggest barrier. You hear folks (many of whom may not know any more than you, believe it or not!) throwing around these arcane phrases, and you feel as though you're missing out on most of the conversation. You're afraid to open your mouth for fear of revealing your ignorance.

Well, this book is meant to help. We've done our best to collect as many as possible of the words and phrases peculiar to the Mac and to explain them in simple, common-sense terms. Where possible, we've included examples and illustrations, as well as the occasional historical footnote to let you know where some of the quirkier-sounding usages came from.

We hope *The Macintosh Dictionary* will help cut through the confusion and enhance the fun of the Mac.

—*Andy Baird*

How to Use This Dictionary

I know what you're thinking—you don't need any directions for using a dictionary. And you're probably right, so I'll just make a few comments about some of the components of this book.

Pronunciations: Do you like the arcane pronunciation guides you find in dictionaries? Here's one:

$$\text{dik ʃən-ˌâr i}$$

We figured that would be overkill for this dictionary, so we used our own pronunciation guides, which we think are so obvious that I'm not even going to explain them here. We included pronunciations only for words that we thought readers might mispronounce. Whenever an acronym or other group of letters is supposed to be said as a word, we've given the pronunciation. If you see a bunch of capitalized letters (like ADB or NTSC) that have no pronunciation guide, just say the letters. And whether the letters are pronounced separately or together, we let you know what the alphabet soup stands for.

Cross references: An italicized word in an entry has its own definition listed. We didn't italicize every word that had its own entry, because that would make for awkward reading: *"Drag* the *icon* into the *application* on the *desktop* to open the *document,"* for instance. Instead we just flagged the words we thought you might like to look up right away.

Index: Why would you index a dictionary that's already a list of alphabetized words? Well, you wouldn't, and neither would we—at least, not in the normal fashion. So we included a few topical indexes: words that are related, although you might not realize that just from browsing through the dictionary or looking something up. The "words" BTW, OTOH, and IMHO are all telecommunications shorthand, for instance.

What's missing? We didn't have room in this book for everything we thought of—and we probably didn't think of everything, either. Let us know what we missed. Drop us a line on email (you can look that up if you don't know what it is) or through the regular mail.

My email addresses are:

> *CompuServe: 72511,233*
> *America Online: SharonZA*
> *AppleLink: D4957*

Andy's email address is:

> *America Online: AFC Andy*

There's a form at the back of the book you can use for paper mail, if you like; or, just use the address that's on it so you can mail us your own note.

—*Sharon Zardetto Aker*

P.S. About using this dictionary. You can use it like a regular dictionary and look things up when you want a definition. But that's not the only, or necessarily the best, way to use it. Just read it—start to finish, or in any order. You'll pick up all sorts of neat information. And later, you can look up the stuff that you forgot. Just like a real dictionary.

Aa

accelerator An add-on *board* that makes your Mac run faster. This can be an economical way to get more use out of an old Mac instead of trading up to an expensive new model (the way Apple wants you to do). A typical accelerator has a faster *microprocessor,* which takes over from your Mac's original processor.

access privileges On a *network,* where a number of different users may be able to see a shared folder, the folder's access privileges determine whether any given user or group of users will be able to make changes to the files in that folder.

access time The average amount of time (usually in milliseconds) it takes for a hard disk drive to start reading any file. Although it's widely used as a *benchmark* of hard disk speed (often accompanied by weasel words like "effective"), access time actually has relatively little effect on overall speed. What's more important than access time is how fast data can be moved from the hard disk to the Mac and how fast your Mac can deal with the data.

active matrix Describes a type of liquid crystal display *(LCD)* that has a transistor for each *pixel* (unlike passive matrix or *supertwist* displays). Active matrix displays have higher contrast and a wider useful viewing angle, but they're harder to make and cost more. Why are they so hard to make? Well, a 640 x 480 panel has over 300,000 transistors; if even one doesn't work, the panel is unacceptable. Out of every hundred active-matrix displays manufactured, about eighty-five must be discarded for defects. No wonder they're expensive!

ADB Apple Desktop Bus. A system for connecting keyboards, mice, *trackballs, graphics tablets,* and other input devices to the Mac. Older Macs (the Plus and earlier) used a different system, so their keyboards aren't interchangeable with those of newer Macs.

Adobe Adobe Systems, one of three companies at the heart of the desktop publishing revolution. (The other two are *Apple,* builder of Macs and *LaserWriters,* and Aldus, creator of PageMaker.) Adobe's *PostScript* graphical language made it possible to do sophisticated typesetting and graphics on small computers and relatively inexpensive printers. Even more important, it became an industry-wide standard. Nowadays, PostScript can be found on printers ranging from $1,300 to $50,000 in cost, and a PostScript document created for the cheapest of these will print out identically—but at higher resolution, of course—on the most expensive.

Adobe also introduced two trend-setting programs: Illustrator, a PostScript drawing program that revolutionized object-oriented graphics, and Photoshop, an astonishingly powerful photo-retouching and image-processing program that lets a $5,000 Mac do the work of a $100,000 *Scitex* workstation (albeit more slowly). Each of these programs established a new category of software, and was followed by many imitators.

Adobe Type Manager See *ATM.*

AFP AppleTalk Filing Protocol. A standard way of sharing files and programs among users on a *network.* Network software that works this way (not all of it does!) is said to be "AFP compliant," which is a very desirable thing.

alert A message in a small rectangular box that pops up on screen to tell you something important (like "Sorry, but this disk is unreadable. You do have backups, don't you?"). An alert can also be just a beep (you can choose what it sounds like with the Sound control panel).

The file "I Can't Open this File?" could not be opened/printed (the application is busy or missing).

OK

algorithm A step-by-step set of instructions—like a recipe—for processing information from one form to another. For instance, the algorithm "slice thinly, sprinkle with sugar, flour, and cinnamon, place in pastry shell and bake 35 min. at 350° F" can be used to transform apples into pie. In the *HyperTalk* language, the algorithm

```
if month is in "September, April, June, November" then
  put 30 into days
else
  if month is in "February" then
    if year is "leap" then
      put 29 into days
    else
      put 28 into days
    end if
  else
    put 31 into days
  end if
end if
```

converts a month into the number of days it contains.

alias A stand-in for any item on the *desktop*. Opening an alias actually opens the item it stands for. What do you use this for? Well, you can put aliases of all your favorite *applications* into the Apple Menu Items folder. This makes the programs' aliases appear on your Apple menu, but you don't need to put all the programs themselves into the same folder; they can stay in their own folders.

Utilities alias

aliasing A technical term for the stairstep appearance of diagonal lines and curves when seen on a low-*resolution* display. Commonly known as the dreaded *jaggies*.

alpha channel A special *grayscale* version of a graphic image, often used in an advanced image-processing program like Photoshop as a mask to isolate part of the image.

alphanumeric Including both letters and numbers. For example, the alphanumeric keys on your keyboard include all the printable *characters*, but not Shift, Command, Option, function keys, and so on. (IBM devotees like to say "alphameric.")

America Online   See *AOL*.

analog   Used to describe information or signals (such as music) that change smoothly
and continuously, as opposed to *digital*
information, which changes in discrete steps. For an
example of a pure analog device, see *Lava Lite*.

anti-aliasing   A way of hiding *jaggies*
in *bitmap* graphics by putting intermediate color values into adjacent *pixels*.
Easier to show than to explain, it's
simply a way of fooling the eye so that
a low-*resolution* bitmap display looks
smoother than it really is.

AOL   America Online. A commercial *information service* that lets you access large libraries
of useful information, download files, and
communicate with other computer users all
over the country. Broadly similar in purpose
to *CompuServe* and *GEnie*, AOL is distinguished from the
other services by its completely Mac-like user interface,
which lets you do things like open folders and files by
simply double-clicking instead of typing cryptic commands. If you have questions or feedback on this book,
you can send AOL mail to Andy Baird at "AFC Andy" and
to Sharon Aker at "SharonZA".

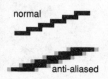

Apple   Originally: a typical Silicon Valley garage
company, founded in 1975 by a couple of hackers
named *Woz* and *Jobs* to sell microcomputer kits. Later: a
wild and crazy computer company that invented the
Macintosh and dragged the whole industry, kicking and
screaming, into the age of graphical *user interfaces*. Currently: a huge, lumbering corporate beast, still blessed
with occasional outbursts of wild and crazy genius. (Thank
goodness!)

AppleEvents   A standard set of messages that one program can send to another, telling the other program to
perform certain common actions. For example, a program

might send a "dosc" (do script) AppleEvent to *HyperCard*, telling it to run a certain *HyperTalk script,* or program.

Apple File Exchange   Included with Apple's system software, this utility program lets you move files from *Apple][* or *DOS* (IBM) floppies onto Mac disks, and vice versa. Unfortunately, it's cursed with a *user interface* so poor it makes DOS software look good.

AppleLink   A proprietary *information service* used by Apple to keep in touch with its dealers, with commercial hardware and software makers, and with *user groups.* To use it, you need an AppleLink account (of course!), Apple's special software, and a *modem.* If you have questions or feedback on this book, you can send AppleLink mail to Sharon Aker at address "D4957."

Apple menu   The little apple in the upper left corner of your screen; you can pull down a menu from it that lists whatever you put into your *Apple Menu Items* folder. The top item on the Apple menu usually tells you about the program you're currently using; it says something like "About MacWhizBang..." A few utilities such as *QuicKeys* or *Suitcase II* may add their own items to the Apple menu.

Apple Menu Items   A special folder inside your *System Folder.* Under *System 7,* any program or *desk accessory* put into this folder is placed on your *Apple menu.* That makes it easy for you to keep your most frequently used tools in one handy place, instead of poking through a bunch of folders every time you want to run a program. Better still, put *aliases* of your programs into the Apple Menu Items folder so that you don't have to move the programs themselves.

AppleShare   A way for Macs on a *network* to share *folders* with each other. A shared folder appears on your Mac's *desktop* and you can open it, use or copy its files, and so on.

AppleTalk   A simple, inexpensive way of connecting several computers so that they can share information and accessories such as printers. A small adapter box plugs into the printer connector in the back of each Mac; then wires connect the boxes together, forming a *network*. The most common use for AppleTalk is to connect Macs to *LaserWriters*.

AppleTalk Remote Access Also referred to as ARA. A nifty way for one *networked* Mac to take control of another. Does that sound sinister? Well, imagine you're at home and get an idea for some changes to a document on your Mac at work. With AppleTalk Remote Access, you can connect to your office network over the phone (using a *modem*) and use your office Mac just as if it were sitting right on your desk at home. Pretty cool!

Apple II (APPLE TWO) One of the first personal computers (introduced in 1976). It's hopelessly underpowered by today's standards, but there are still many in use in schools. The only Apple II hardware still in production is a *coprocessor* board for the Macintosh LC. An Apple II can't run Macintosh programs because it uses a different *microprocessor* from the Macintosh's 68000 family, but you can move documents back and forth between the Mac and the II using *Apple File Exchange*.

application Any computer program you can run by double-clicking its icon on the *desktop*. Applications are most often used as tools (like a *word processor* or a graphics program) to create and edit documents.

application memory The section of *memory* (*RAM*) that is available to a program—its private playpen, you might say. This value can be set from the program's *Get Info* box (available from the *desktop*). If a program tells you it's running out of memory, one thing you can do is quit, increase its application memory, and then run it again. (Also sometimes referred to as a program's memory allocation or *MultiFinder* partition.)

application menu A menu on the right side of your screen that lists the *applications* currently running, and lets you switch from one to another. The application menu is always headed by a shrunken *icon* of the program currently in use.

architecture A vague term for "the way it's put together"; the structure of a computer (hardware architecture) or a program (software architecture). A "closed" architecture (as in the original Mac) means it's hard to add or change anything; an "open" architecture (much talked about nowadays) makes expansion relatively easy.

archive A place where you store seldom-used documents. In Mac parlance, an archive is a special document that contains files that have been compressed with a utility like *StuffIt*. Several related files (for example, a program and its online documentation) can be compressed into one archive, with a tremendous reduction in size.

Archive.sit

argument An input value that's passed to a program. For example, the *HyperTalk* command "subtract…from" takes two arguments, as in "Subtract 5 from age", where the arguments are "5" and "age".

ascender The tall part of a lowercase letter (like "h" or "k") that sticks up above the average height of lowercase letters (the *x height*).

ASCII (ASS KEE) American Standard Code for Information Interchange. A system used by all modern microcomputers in which each character is represented by a number. For example, A is 65, an exclamation point is 33, and a carriage return is 13. There are 256 possible ASCII codes, but only 96 are printing characters; the rest are nonprinting control functions such as the carriage return and tab. Apple uses many of the higher ASCII codes for special characters like • and ≈.

Atkinson, Bill One of the true geniuses of the Mac, shy but brilliant Bill Atkinson gave us *QuickDraw*, the *Toolbox* routines that handle all graphics displayed on the Mac; MacPaint, the first Mac graphics program; *HyperCard*, the breakthrough that made it possible for anyone to create Mac programs—and lots of other goodies along the way. Bill is now working at General Magic, an Apple-subsidized company where he and other Mac wizards like *Andy Hertzfeld* are creating a revolutionary *palmtop* computer system.

ATM Adobe Type Manager. An *outline font* technology built into the Macintosh *operating system* in versions 7.1 and later, ATM offers better-looking text on the screen when using *PostScript* typefaces. ATM also lets inexpensive non-PostScript printers (like Hewlett-Packard's DeskWriter) produce high-quality output at any type size. (Similar advantages are offered by Apple's *TrueType* technology, but TrueType uses fonts that are not compatible with the PostScript standard or ATM.)

authoring system A programming language with all the trimmings. This phrase usually describes a collection of tools that make it easier for folks who aren't heavy-duty programmers to create *applications*—most often for educational or *multimedia* purposes. Good examples are *HyperCard*, MacroMedia Director, and AuthorWare.

A/UX An alternative to the standard Mac *operating system*; it's Apple's version of *Unix*, a *multitasking* operating system developed at Bell Labs back in the sixties. A/UX is Apple's attempt to sugar-coat the notoriously hostile Unix *user interface*, famous for cryptic commands like grep, dis, and wc. It requires heavy-duty hardware, great gobs of *RAM* and hard disk space, and is "mostly" compatible with standard Mac *applications*. Not surprisingly, only about one Mac in a hundred uses it.

Bb

background Describes an activity that goes on "behind the scenes" while you're working on something else. For example, *PrintMonitor's* background printing lets you continue to edit your file or even work in an entirely different program while a document is being sent to the printer.

back up To make a copy of a file or set of files for safekeeping. Information on computer disks is easily damaged, either by physical abuse (such as spilled coffee, nearby magnets, or heat), by a malfunctioning program, or by invisible, mischievous gremlins who tend to congregate in the vicinity of someone working late on an especially crucial job. It's very important to make backups of your files regularly. Inexpensive commercial programs make this a fast, easy process even for those with large hard disks. Five minutes a day spent backing up your disk can save you the agony of losing many hours of work to an unexpected crash. If you're a procrastinator, you might try this exercise: pretend your hard disk just became unreadable. How many days of work have you lost? Right. Now go do a backup!

balloon help Those cute little comic-strip balloons that pop up wherever your *pointer* is; they explain the various parts of a program's *user interface*, such as its pushbuttons and menus.

> This is an entry in the Macintosh Dictionary.

bandwidth The amount of information that can be handled by a device or system. For example, a telephone can carry audio signals only in a band between about 20 Hz and 4,000 Hz—just enough for intelligible speech, but no good for music. This is a low-bandwidth system. On the other hand, a cable TV system may use signals up to 400,000,000 Hz—it takes that much bandwidth to carry dozens of TV channels. In general, the broader the bandwidth of a system, the more information it can carry, the faster it can carry it—and the more it costs.

baseline The imaginary line on which the bottoms of most letters rest. Some letters (like "g," "j," and "p") have parts called *descenders* that extend below the baseline.

Boy

BASIC (BASIC) Beginner's All-purpose Symbolic Instruction Code. A sixties-vintage computer language once popular with novices. Now largely superseded in the Mac world by *HyperTalk,* which is easier to use and can do more. Sometimes referred to as *"Fortran* for idiots," BASIC is still the standard language for many *DOS* users.

batch processing As in baking cookies at home, this means doing things one batch at a time—as opposed to making cookies in a factory, where they move continuously down a conveyor belt. The phrase usually refers to something that happens automatically to a series of files— for example, automatically translating a group of Word-Perfect documents to MacWrite format.

baud Used loosely to mean bits per second; a measurement of how fast computer data can be sent over a *serial* connection (as when using a *modem* to communicate over the phone lines). 2400 baud, a commonly used speed, is roughly equivalent to 240 *characters* per second. The unit is named after the French engineer Baudot.

Baudot (BAH DOE) A standard (like *ASCII)* for encoding and transmitting letters and numbers. Created by the French engineer for whom it's named, this old system has a very limited character set and certain Gallic idiosyncrasies about its codings. Each character is specified by 6 bits, and data is transmitted at 45.5 or 50 baud—dismally slow by today's standards.

Although long obsolete in the computer world, Baudot is still very widely used by hundreds of thousands of deaf people, whose TDDs (Telecommunication Devices for the Deaf) rely on this standard. Some diehard radio amateurs also use Baudot for radioteletype (RTTY) communication.

In both cases, the original reason for choosing this technologically inferior system was the ready availability of obsolete Baudot-standard teletype equipment at bargain prices.

BBS Bulletin Board System. A computer connected to a phone line so that other computers can communicate with it, a BBS serves as a common meeting place, a mail stop, and a data library. You need two things to connect to a BBS with your Mac: a *modem*, so that your computer can communicate over the phone, and a terminal *emulator* program, which lets your computer talk to a different computer in a way the other machine can understand.

Thousands of BBSs exist; most are single-computer operations run from private homes. Many BBSs are devoted to specialized areas of interest: there are boards for writers, photographers, shortwave listeners, and scores of other hobbies and professions.

bells and whistles Features, often superfluous ones, as in, "I just need a good basic printer; I don't want to pay for all the bells and whistles."

benchmark A standardized task used as a test, usually of speed. For example, a common benchmark of *microprocessor* speed is the "Sieve of Eratosthenes" *algorithm* for finding prime numbers. Running this program on several different computers, stopwatch in hand, gives you a rough way to compare the speed of the hardware. The key word here is "rough"; benchmark comparisons are notoriously slippery, because different computers excel at different tasks—a machine that's very fast at integer math may be a sluggard when it comes to *floating-point* calculations. Microprocessor makers like Intel and Motorola are famous for volleying carefully tailored benchmarks back and forth to prove that one chip is faster than another.

beta testing A stage of software development roughly equivalent to "not ready for prime time." When a program is first created, it is tested in-house by its developers; this is called "alpha testing." β

11

However, finding bugs in something you programmed yourself is like trying to proofread your own writing—you never catch all the mistakes. The next stage is to let a selected group of outsiders use the program.

These folks, called beta testers, wring out the product and find hordes of *bugs* its creators never even dreamed of; they also offer suggestions about desirable features. Usually a program goes through several beta versions, each one incorporating bug fixes and improvements suggested by the beta testers. Although the testers are sworn to secrecy, traditionally someone leaks information about the program to *MacWeek*, which regularly publishes "sneak preview" articles. When most or all of the bugs seem to be gone, the program is released commercially. The beta testers usually receive a free copy of the final version as a reward for their labors.

Caution: if you see a version number like 2.0b3, that "b" means it's a beta version, so you beta beware of bugs! And "d" versions (like 3.0d9) are even worse—they're development (alpha) versions, guaranteed to have more bugs than an ant farm.

Bézier curve (BAYZ YAY) A mathematical curve defined by several "control points" that mark its start and end points and determine its shape. Because they can draw just about any two-dimensional shape, Bézier curves are used by the *PostScript* graphical language to create all kinds of shapes, including letters, numbers, and other *characters*.

Big Blue A common nickname for *IBM*, inspired by the company's blue logo.

binary A value expressed in the base-2 number system, where the only possible digits are 1 and 0. Since these can be represented by "on" and "off" in an electronic circuit, it's a good system for computers to use. But don't worry—you don't need to understand that $10 + 10 = 100$ (the binary way of saying $2 + 2 = 4$) to use your Mac!

BinHex (BINN HEX) BINary to HEXadecimal. A program long obsolete in most parts of the world, it converts *binary* values to *hexadecimal* values so that a file can be transmitted to another computer. Users of technologically primitive *networks* like the *Internet* are still forced to employ this 1985-vintage utility every time they want to transfer a file. The rest of us don't need to be bothered, thank goodness! A file whose name ends in .HCX or .HEX is a BinHex file.

bit BInary digiT. The smallest unit of information in a computer; it can be either 0 (off) or 1 (on). We don't talk about bits much these days; pretty much everything is done in *bytes,* which are 8 bits long.

bitmap A two-dimensional array of dots that forms an image or a *character* (think of a picture made by blackening certain squares on a sheet of graph paper). Bitmapped graphics and text have fixed *resolutions,* unlike *object-oriented* graphics. Thus, a curve drawn as a bitmap looks exactly as jagged on screen at 72 dots per inch (dpi) as when printed out on a 300-dpi *LaserWriter.* Examples of bitmapped graphics applications are MacPaint and Photoshop.

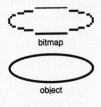

bitmap

object

bleed To run off the edge of a page; said of a photo or graphic. "The mug shot bleeds left on this page" is printer's jargon meaning that the portrait in question extends all the way to the left edge, with no border on that side. "Full bleed" means that an image extends to all four edges.

blessed folder That fortunate *folder* holding the sacred *System* files that your Mac is currently using; you can recognize it by the tiny Mac icon it bears. Why is this important? If you have just one *System Folder,* then by definition it's blessed. But if you're foolish enough to have several System Folders on the same disk, only one can be in control at a given time. That folder is the blessed folder, and is the only one to carry the mini-Mac icon.

System Folder

Woe betide him who shall suffer multiple System Folders to dwell on the selfsame disk! For they shall contend amongst themselves for control, *munging* your directories and wreaking havoc upon your files. Be ye therefore warned, and guard diligently against this dread happenstance.

board Synonymous with *card*.

bomb To fail catastrophically—usually without warning and at the worst possible time (like just before that big presentation for the Board of Directors). See *crash* for the gruesome details.

Boolean Having to do with binary logic—that AND/OR/NOT stuff that comes in so handy when you're searching for something. For example, a *database* program's search function might let you look for all customer records in which the state is "New Jersey" OR "NJ". Or you might want to locate all the UPI news stories that contain the word "conspiracy" but NOT "CIA". These are Boolean functions, and they let you narrow down your searches to focus on just what you want (like recipes with chocolate AND almonds but NOT coconut). Boolean logic is named, logically enough, for George Boole, a nineteenth century English mathematician whose discoveries paved the way for modern digital electronics.

boot blocks Some special information at the beginning of a disk (hard or floppy) that tells the Mac how to *boot up* (start up). You can't see them ordinarily, and you don't even need them unless the disk has a *System Folder* on it, but on rare occasions the boot blocks may become corrupted and need to be rewritten; the *formatter* program that came with your hard disk drive can do this.

boot up To start up your computer (that is, turn on the power and, if you don't have a hard disk, insert a floppy with a *System Folder* on it). This odd-sounding bit of jargon dates back to the very early days of computing, when starting up was a complicated process. Early computers had no *ROM*, or permanent memory. When you first turned on the power,

14

the machine contained no program to tell it what to do—it was truly a blank slate.

To start up one of these old machines, you had to first enter a short "loader" program (in *binary*) by flipping switches; this program was just sufficient to let the machine use its paper tape or punched card reader to load in a longer, full-fledged loader program, which in turn could be used to load the program you wanted to run! Loading a loader in order to load the loader that would load your program reminded operators of the old phrase "Pulling yourself up by your own bootstraps"; hence, the short loader came to be called a bootstrap loader, and the whole process, "booting up."

bps bits per second. A measure of how fast data is being sent over a network or other computer-to-computer connection.

bridge A box linking two computer *networks* together; a type of *router*.

BTW By The Way. *Telecommunications* shorthand.

buffer A temporary storage area in your computer's *RAM* (memory). The *Disk Cache* is an example of a buffer that temporarily stores information read in from a disk drive. Your Mac also has an event buffer that stores input events like keystrokes and mouse clicks as they occur. Thanks to the event buffer, nothing gets lost, even if the Mac is too busy to display a keystroke at the moment you type it.

bug Unexpected behavior usually caused by a mistake in programming but sometimes by a hardware malfunction. According to the late computer pioneer Grace Murray Hopper, the first computer bug was just that—a moth that became stuck in one of the relays of the Mark I, a very early (forties vintage) electromechanical computer, causing it to malfunction.

buggy Prone to malfunction. Examples: Apple's System 6.0, *Quark XPress*, and the *ImageWriter LQ* printer.

bullet A large black dot (•) used to draw attention to items on a list. Folks who don't know any better sometimes substitute a lowercase "o" or an asterisk, but all Mac users know that typing Option-8 will get you a nice bullet in practically any Mac typeface. You did know that, didn't you? See *option characters* for some other useful symbols you may not have noticed.

bulletin board system See *BBS*.

bundled Included. In the computer business, this usually refers to software that is included when you buy hardware. For example, when the Mac was first introduced, it came bundled with the MacWrite *word processor* and MacPaint graphics program. If it hadn't, there wouldn't have been much you could do but admire the Finder's desktop display, since there was no other application software when the Mac came out!

bus Not the kind you ride on, but an electrical circuit that lets differ- ent devices (such as plug-in *NuBus* cards or *SCSI* hard disks) share 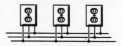 information through a common set of wires. For example, all the outlets on one circuit in your house are connected by a simple three-wire bus; each device you plug in is connected to every other device by the same three wires, which they all share.

byte A unit of information in a computer's memory or disk drive; each byte holds one *character*. A byte contains 8 *bits*, or *binary* digits—or 2 "nybbles," if you want to be technical, but nobody talks about nybbles these days.

Cc

C A computer language used to create the majority of Macintosh programs now on the market; C is cryptic and difficult for beginners, but yields fast, compact programs. Developed at Bell Labs, where it replaced—you guessed it—"B." (Those guys hated unnecessary typing, so everything they created had a very short name. See *A/UX* for more examples.)

cables These snakes in the grass of modern computing take a big bite out of our national productivity. Knowledgeable authorities estimate that over 3.6 zillion hours are wasted each year in the US alone by people looking for the right cables to connect computer equipment together. The only beneficiaries are the companies who make the cables (in a staggering profusion of types). Take a tip from me: If you want to make money in this racket, don't build computers—build cables! Computers come and go, but cables are an eternal necessity.

cache (CASH, not CA SHAY!) A part of *RAM* (memory) that's set aside to store information temporarily. Macs can use caches in several ways:

1) The Disk Cache holds data read in from your disk. The next time your program needs that particular piece of information, it's able to fetch it from the cache much more quickly than if it had to go to the disk to get it, because RAM is thousands of times faster than a hard disk. However, since the cache sets aside memory for itself that your programs can't use, it may prevent certain programs from running. The Disk Cache size can be adjusted from the Memory *control panel;* 128K is a good all-around value.

Cache Size [192K]

2) The 68020, 68030, and 68040 *microprocessors* have instruction and data caches built into the microprocessor

17

chip. This speeds things up, but a few programs may have problems with this arrangement; you may need to turn the caches off (from a control panel) to make some programs work properly.

3) Programs such as Adobe Type Manager *(ATM)* can set up RAM caches to hold their own information temporarily. In general, the larger you make such a cache, the faster the program works—but the less memory you have left over for other programs to use.

CAD/CAM Computer Aided Design/Computer Aided Manufacturing. A catchall category that includes many different programs. Some examples: drafting programs (PowerDraw, for instance); architectural modeling programs; engineering applications that calculate stress on a girder of a particular size; plus the programs that control automatic milling machines, lathes, and robotic arms.

camera-ready copy A piece of artwork or text that's ready to be photographed and made into an offset printing plate. This used to be done with wax, X-Acto knives, and Rubylith; now it all can be done on the Mac and printed on a laser printer or *imagesetter*.

card A printed circuit board, which usually plugs into an expansion *slot*. "Just pop this card into your IIci, and you'll be running twice as fast!"

Carousel Adobe's universal document interchange standard. This PostScript-based technology allows users to exchange and edit documents, even though they may have neither the programs that originally created them nor the special fonts they contain. How can they do it? By using the chameleon-like abilities of *Multiple Masters* PostScript fonts to emulate the size, weight, and general appearance of the missing fonts. If Adobe succeeds in making this an industry-wide standard (and they have a good shot at it), this will make it possible for a huge variety of computers and programs to seamlessly exchange documents of all sorts, removing one of our major headaches.

carpal tunnel syndrome An all too common occupational disease caused by too much typing, mousing, or other repetitive hand motion. Symptoms: shooting pains or numbness in the wrist, hand, or thumb joints. Cause: the nerves from the hand pass through the wrist bones in a channel called the carpal 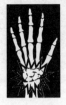 tunnel; repetitive hand motions can cause pinched or even permanently damaged nerves. Cure: prevention is best—use wrist rests, take frequent breaks, vary your tasks. Severe cases may require surgery.

One common early warning sign is waking up at night with a tingling in your wrist or hand. CTS can be permanently disabling, so if you start to experience symptoms like this, don't wait to see whether it'll go away on its own! Change your habits now to prevent trouble later. If you suspect you may have CTS, see your doctor before it's too late and you end up spending the rest of your life wearing a wrist brace.

CCITT Consultative Committee on International Telephone and Telegraph. An organization that sets worldwide standards for things like data and voice transmission. They're best known in the Mac world for the *V.32* and *V.42* family of *modem* standards.

cdev (SEE DEV) The old word for a *control panel*.

CD-I Compact Disc-Interactive. A system that puts computer programs, sound, and graphics (including moving video and digitized photos) on a disc similar to a compact digital audio disc (CD). A special player is required, and the images are displayed on your television or video *monitor*. CD-I was developed by Philips (inventors of the audio cassette, compact disc, and *LaserDisc*) for use in *interactive* applications like games, education, and training. Similar technology is used in Intel's *DVI* system.

CD-ROM (SEE DEE ROMM) Compact Disc–Read Only Memory. A disc that looks exactly like a compact audio disc (CD) but is used to store a mixture of digital audio and computer information. A CD-ROM can hold five or six hundred megabytes of information, which is equal to 750,000 floppy disks! (CD-ROM is unrelated to *ROM* memory chips.)

There are two big differences between CD-ROMs and hard disks or floppies: 1) CD-ROMs, like CDs, can't be recorded on by the user (that's why they're called "read only"); 2) because they're much slower than hard disks, it takes much longer to find and read the data you're looking for. So, this medium is best suited to publishing large reference works like encyclopedias and service manuals.

center tab A tab character that causes text to be centered on the tab's location.

Centronics In common usage, a type of printer *interface* used by *DOS* computers. Actually, Centronics was a US printer manufacturer that dominated the market until the Japanese took over and left its name on this parallel interface standard.

CGM Computer Graphics Metafile. One of many "standard" formats for graphics files on *DOS* computers. CGM can include *bitmaps, vector* graphics, or both.

character A letter, number, symbol, or punctuation mark that can be displayed on your screen or printed out. It is represented by 8 *bits*, or 1 *byte*, in your computer.

check box A small, square button, normally found in groups, that lets you pick as many choices as you want from a number of choices. The check box has an "X" in it if it's chosen.

Check as many as you wish:
- ☒ money
- ☒ romance
- ☒ fame

Chimes of Doom (Also known as the Heavenly Chords of Doom.) Normally, Mac II family machines chime once on startup (older Macs just beep). If, however, you hear an arpeggiated chord (or chords), it's a signal that you have serious problems: a bad *NuBus board*, a *SCSI* conflict, an improperly installed or loose *SIMM*, or some other hardware malfunction. The chimes contain coded information

C

about what the problem is—for example, which memory bank is bad. If you were a musician with perfect pitch, you just might be able to figure out what the various chords mean—that is, if they were documented in your owner's manual, which they aren't. All you can tell is that you've got serious trouble when you hear them.

Who knows? Maybe Apple was looking forward to the day when all their documentation would be in multimedia form when they came up with this dumb idea. Or maybe they just wanted to make it hard for tone-deaf people to work with Macs.

chip An integrated circuit (IC) containing several thousand extremely tiny transistors etched into the surface of a thin slice of silicon about the size of your little fingernail. The chip is enclosed in a plastic or ceramic package with dozens of metal "pins" or contacts. Most ICs look like big black centipedes with shiny metal legs.

Chooser A program on your *Apple menu* that lets you choose which *networked* printer you want to send your output to, or which *AppleTalk zone* you want to be connected to.

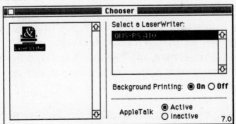

chroma key To merge two video images so that one image shows up only where there is a certain key color in the other. (For chroma keying to be possible, the two video signals must be *genlocked* in perfect synchronization.)

21

For example, a TV weather person is photographed stand-ing in front of a blue screen, while another camera points at a weather map. The two signals are combined by special chroma keying circuitry so that wherever the blue appears, the map will show through, thereby creating the illusion that the person is standing in front of a large map. (Of course, if she's wearing a blue scarf, the map will show through that as well, producing a very peculiar effect: a person with a large hole in her neck!)

Frequently used for special effects, chroma keying is also commonly used to combine computer-generated graphics such as titles with live video.

CIS CompuServe Information Service. (In view of CompuServe's high prices, some folks spell it "CI$.") See *CompuServe*.

Claris The amazing corporate yo-yo of the computer indus-try, Claris was spun off by Apple several years ago, then suddenly reeled back in. Claris was created in an attempt to deflect criticism that Apple was creating too many applications like *HyperCard*, MacWrite, and MacDraw, thus competing with smaller software publishers. The company was supposed to become a fully independent entity over a period of several years, but Apple got cold feet when Claris began making noises about creating programs for other computers besides the Mac (meaning IBM PCs, of course)—and so Claris was made a wholly owned subsid-iary again. (At that point, most of Claris' top management quit in disgust.) Claris currently publishes such major programs as ClarisWorks, MacWrite, MacDraw Pro, Claris CAD, HyperCard, FileMaker Pro, and Resolve. Its relationship with Apple remains ambiguous, but there's more than a hint of incest.

Classic Small, inexpensive Mac. See *Macintosh*.

clip art Images meant for general purpose use: things like Santas, Easter bunnies, Macs, and decorative borders, that can be used in your greet-ing cards and newsletters. *HyperCard* comes with a variety of *bitmapped* clip art; if you use a *LaserWriter* or other *PostScript* printer, high-quality Encapsulated PostScript *(EPS)* clip art is available both commercially and from most *user groups*.

Clipboard A temporary storage area in your Mac's memory (also sometimes a file in your *System Folder)* that holds text, pictures, or anything else you want to move from one program or document to another. When you Clipboard
select something and choose the Edit menu commands *Cut* or *Copy,* your selection is placed in the Clipboard; when you paste, the contents of the Clipboard are copied into your document.

One thing you should know: when you copy something to the Clipboard and then go to another program to paste it, some formatting information may be lost. Text, for example, will lose its font and style attributes; *PostScript* graphics become plain old *PICTs,* and so forth. The Clipboard is useful, but it isn't perfect.

The Clipboard can hold only one thing at a time; when you copy or cut, the new item replaces whatever was there. The Clipboard is saved if you quit one program and move to another, but the Clipboard's contents are forgotten when you turn off your Mac.

clock speed How fast your computer computes is partly determined by how fast its *microprocessor* runs; that's controlled by the speed of the processor's clock, a metronome-like signal that synchronizes the orderly march of data and instructions through the computer. Since it costs more to make microprocessor *chips* that run at higher clock speeds, fast computers are generally more expensive than slow ones. Clock speeds are given in megahertz *(MHz);* typical numbers are in the 16–50 MHz range.

clone Something so similar to the original that it's the same for all practical purposes—for example, an inexpensive computer that's compatible with a more expensive name-brand model. Not necessarily just a cheap substitute, a clone may even be faster than the original model. Common in the IBM world, clones are almost unavailable for the Macintosh—the closest thing is the *Outbound* portable.

close box The small square at the upper right of most Macintosh windows that lets you put away, or close, a window.

clut (CLUT) Color Look-Up Table. In Macs with 8-bit *color* displays, where only 256 colors can be displayed at one time out of the sixteen million possibilities allowed by the Mac's *operating system*, the System uses a color look-up table to decide which 256 colors will be used with a given program or document. The clut (technically, a *resource* of type 'clut') is attached to a document; changing the clut or displaying an image with the wrong clut can lead to spectacular and sometimes hideous results. (Color *paint programs* often call the clut a color *palette.)*

CMYK Cyan/Magenta/Yellow/blacK. The four colors of ink commonly used in color printing; also called *process colors*. By combining these four, a wide range of colors can be obtained.

coaxial cable A type of electrical cable used for signals that are especially susceptible to interference; a common example is the cable used for cable TV. It consists of an insulated inner wire, a tubular outer shield (usually made from fine braided wire) that completely surrounds it, and an outer insulating jacket. The outer shield protects the inner wire from picking up or radiating electrical noise. Coaxial cable, usually called coax (CO AX) for short, is also used for *Ethernet networks*.

code Slang for "computer program," so called because it's written in a language indecipherable to the uninitiated.

collapse The opposite of *expand;* to hide the lower levels of an outline view. For example:

1) In a text-view Finder window, to hide the contents of a folder by clicking on the triangle to the left of its name.

2) To display an *outliner* document with only its major headings showing; a good way to get an overview without becoming bogged down in details.

color A big subject, no? Don't worry, I won't try to cover it all here! But let's talk about the possible kinds of color you'll find on the Mac. They're named by how many *bits* are assigned to each *pixel*. Why should we care about that? Well, the more bits, the more colors a pixel can have. For example:

1-bit color Since a bit can have only two possible states—on and off—it's not surprising that a display with 1-bit color can show only two "colors": black and white. Small Macs like the Classic have 1-bit displays.

4-bit color Four bits per pixel make possible sixteen colors ($2^4 = 16$, if you're mathematically minded). Many *DOS* computers use this scheme, but it's far too limiting for Mac users, so you'll practically never see it. (You will, however, see 4-bit *grayscale* from a lot of older *scanners.)*

8-bit color By far the most common arrangement for color Macs, this lets you have 256 different colors ($2^8 = 256$). That sounds like a lot of colors, but the real world is much more subtle than that. To show really photographic images, you need 24-bit color.

24-bit color 24 bits per pixel give you a staggering 16,777,216 colors (2^{24}) to choose from! Serious graphic artists depend on 24-bit displays for photo-retouching and painting. The penalty: the more bits per pixel, the more memory you need—and the longer it takes to get anything done! As a result, the demand for faster Macs and faster video boards has skyrocketed.

32-bit color You get the same number of colors—roughly 16.7 million—as with 24-bit color, but the extra 8 bits are used as an *alpha channel* to determine transparency, or for other specialized functions.

color seps   Color *separations;* a printers' term for separate master documents prepared for each of several colors to be printed.

Command key   The key with the funny symbol variously described as a cloverleaf, propeller, pretzel, or butterfly. (The symbol was originally used in a Swedish tourist guidebook to indicate "something special.") Because they sound similar, the Command key is easy to confuse with the *Control key*, but they do different things. You'll be using the Command key a lot more often.

command-line interface   The way in which users controlled most computers until the Mac came along. A command-line driven computer is strictly text-based; it prompts you for an input (with something like ? or C>), and you type a command like DIR for "Show me the contents of this directory." If you fail to spell or punctuate the command exactly the way the computer wants it, you get an error message like "Unrecognized command." (This happens a lot.) Command-line interfaces also tend to assume that you know exactly what you're doing. If you type "DEL *.*", the computer cheerfully erases every last file on your hard disk, without bothering to ask whether you really wanted to do that! The command-line interface is obviously clumsy and user-hostile, but amazingly, it's still used on millions of *DOS* computers around the world.

An extreme example of a command-line *interface* was the original version of the widely used dBASE program. When you started the program (by typing "DBASE"), it opened with a perfectly blank screen showing only one character: a period (the famous dBASE "dot prompt"). No menus, no tool palettes, no windows with title bars—just a dot. It was entirely up to you to look up what commands were available and figure out what to type in, and heaven help you if you spelled it wrong!

compatibility A mythical state of bliss, often spoken of but seldom achieved: the ability to work harmoniously with other hardware or software. For example, Macintosh software is usually compatible with Macintoshes, while *DOS* software is occasionally compatible with DOS computers.

C

compiler A program for creating programs, which takes a series of commands (called source code) written in a computer language like *C* or *Fortran* and converts it into the *binary* numbers (called object code) that a *microprocessor* can understand. Why is the translation process necessary? Well, if you had to write 1101 0011 0001 0011 1110 every time you wanted to add two numbers together, you'd be pretty unhappy! A compiler lets you write "Add 1 to 2"; then it does the hard part. (For another way of creating programs, see *interpreter.*)

composite video A video signal in which all the color and synchronization information has been combined into one signal, with a resulting sacrifice in overall quality. The "video out" RCA jack on a typical VCR carries a composite video signal. A better way to transmit video is with *RGB* signals, where the information is kept separate. Color Mac displays use the RGB method.

CompuServe A large computer *information service* with hundreds of thousands of subscribers. You can call CompuServe with your computer and a *modem* connected to your phone. For an hourly fee, you can download free programs, read the news from various wire services, track your investments, shop, send mail, ask for help with computer problems, and much more. There's a sign-up fee and a monthly charge as well as the hourly usage fee. Other similar services are *GEnie* and *America Online*. If you have questions or feedback on this book, you can send CompuServe mail to Sharon Aker at address 72511,233. Andy thinks CIS is too user-hostile and too expensive, so he has no account.

computer A high-speed idiot. It can't really do much besides turn bits on and off—but what it does, it does so fast that you'd almost think it was smart if you didn't know better!

concatenate To string together. For example, if you concatenate "ABCD" with "XYZ," the result is "ABCDXYZ."

condensed Opposite of *extended:* a horizontally compressed typeface.

contiguous Adjacent; in reference to *RAM (memory).* For example, a parking lot might have one hundred spaces, of which only seventy-five are filled. But because the cars are parked at random, the largest contiguous group of spaces might be five in a row over in the far corner. Similarly, when you're trying to run several programs under *System 7,* what counts is not the total amount of RAM, but the largest chunk of contiguous RAM available. This is the "Largest Unused Block" the Finder shows you when you pull down the *Apple menu* and choose "About This Macintosh...."

continuous tone A *grayscale* or color image (such as an original photograph), as opposed to a *halftoned* or *dithered* image, which is made up of only one to four discrete ink colors. The only Mac printers capable of creating true continuous tone images are the costly *dye-sublimation* printers. Even super-expensive high-resolution *imagesetters* can't really print true continuous-tone pictures, although the black dots they make are so fine that they can sometimes fool the eye into thinking it's seeing continuous tones.

Control key A *modifier key* at the left of your keyboard that can be used with some applications for special functions; in the Chicago font it can be used to type the Apple, diamond, checkmark, and command symbols. Don't confuse it with the nearby *Command key,* which is more frequently used. (Older Mac keyboards have no Control key.)

control panel A mini-program that lets you change and customize various aspects of your Mac. You can change the volume level, set the clock, adjust *mouse tracking*, and so on with control panels. You store them in the *Control Panels* folder in your *System Folder* and access them from your *Apple menu.*

General Controls

C

Control Panels A special folder inside your *System Folder.* Under System 7, any *control panel* put into this folder will be available when you choose the Control Panels command under the *Apple menu.*

coprocessor A *microprocessor* that works alongside your regular microprocessor to share the load and make things go faster. Examples are the 68881 and 68882 numeric coprocessors, which speed up certain mathematical operations tremendously, and the 80386 coprocessor *boards,* which can be used to let your Mac run *DOS* programs just like an *IBM PC* or PC *clone.*

copy A command on the Edit menu that lets you copy something you've selected to the Clipboard, leaving the selection unchanged. You can then *paste* it somewhere else.

copy protection A way for software publishers to make sure that you don't "share" a program with your friends and cheat the program's authors out of the money they would have made if your friends had bought their own copies. Copy protection is usually accomplished by various tricky bits of programming, all of which at best make life annoying for the honest user, and at worst can cause all kinds of unexplained misbehavior. For these reasons copy protection is uncommon these days—at least in the US. Europe is another story.

cpu central processing unit. An old synonym for *microprocessor;* this is also sometimes used for the box that contains the computer's "guts," as in, "You can set the *monitor* on top of the cpu and save desk space that way."

cracker 1) Someone who illegally invades another's computer system, usually via *modem,* for either mischief or profit. For example, a person who breaks into TRW's credit information system using a forged password, obtains valid credit card numbers, and posts them on a *BBS*.

2) A tool used for prying open the case of a compact Mac (Plus, SE, or Classic).

crash Synonymous with *bomb*. Happens when a program malfunctions so badly that it stops working. The result is usually an *alert* box saying "The program has unexpectedly quit"; or in extreme cases, a *pointer* that won't move, assorted funny noises, or screen garbage. Programs crash (usually) because the programmer made a mistake or (rarely) because the computer's hardware is sick. When this happens, first try holding down Option and Command while pressing the Escape key; under System 7, that will often let you quit to the *Finder*. If that doesn't work, you'll have to push the *reset switch* or turn off the power and turn it on again. A program that crashes can't hurt your Mac, but it can damage information stored on your disk. If that happens, you'll need to use an application like Disk First Aid (free with your system software) or the Norton Utilities (commercial) to recover your damaged files.

CRC Cyclic Redundancy Check. An automatic way of making sure that information you send over the phone lines reaches its destination intact. *Terminal emulator* programs offer this as part of the *XMODEM* file transfer *protocol*.

creator A piece of information that tells what program created a document (normally hidden from the user). For example, all MacPaint files have a creator of MPNT. Ordinarily you'll never see this bit of esoterica, but programs like *ResEdit* can be used to view and change a file's creator if necessary.

CRT Cathode Ray Tube. A commonly used name for the picture tube in a television set or a computer display. The luminous picture on the CRT's screen is "painted" by a beam of electrons emitted by the tube's negatively charged

C

cathode. Back before electrons were well understood, this beam was said to be made of "cathode rays," whence the name.

curly quotes The curved, paired quotation marks (" ") you see in magazines and books like this one, as opposed to the inch marks (") some people still use. Listen, folks, that was fine when typewriters were all we had, but we don't have to do that anymore—the Mac is not a typewriter, you know! (Hey, sounds like a good title for a book.) To get curly quotes, hold down the *Option* key and press [or].

cursor The pointer that moves around the screen when you move the mouse. Different cursor shapes tell you different things about what's going on. For example, the wristwatch cursor means "be patient—I'm working on it"; the *I-beam* cursor means you're ready to edit some text. Sometimes folks mistakenly refer to the *insertion point* as a cursor, but that has a completely different function. Just remember: the cursor always moves with the mouse; the insertion point never moves unless you type or click somewhere.

cut A command on the Edit menu that lets you move something you've selected to the Clipboard, deleting the selection. You can then *paste* it somewhere else.

cyan (SY EN) Blue-green; one of the four *process colors* used in color printing.

Dd

DA Abbreviation for *desk accessory.*

daisychain To connect a string of devices together one after another; something you do when connecting *SCSI* devices together, for example.

DAL (DAHL) Data Access Language. A standard computer language intended to let Macintosh programs get information from *mainframe databases;* frees users from facing the daunting complexity of the mainframe data structures themselves.

DAT (DAT) Digital Audio Tape. A small tape cassette originally intended for recording music, adapted for use as a *backup* device with Macs. A DAT drive can hold well over a billion *bytes* of information, so you can back up very large *hard disks* to DAT cassettes. Like all tape devices, however, DATs are comparatively slow, so you can't substitute one for a hard disk in normal use.

database 1) An organized collection of information, such as names, addresses, phone numbers, order numbers, stock numbers, and inventory levels.

2) A program such as FileMaker that manages databases.

data fork Okay, it's pretty esoteric, but you just might run into this weird-sounding phrase sometime. No, it has nothing to do with eating utensils! It  refers to the part of a Macintosh file that's just plain data (for example, the text of a MacWrite document) as opposed to the file's *resource* fork, which includes things like the icons and sounds added to a *HyperCard* stack.

A given file may have either a data fork, a resource fork, or both. Typically, documents always have data and may also have resources; *applications* always have resources and may also have data. Normally, you won't ever see the two forks as separate entities, but they're there behind the scenes.

date stamp To mark a file with the date on which it was created or modified. The *Finder* does this, making it easy for you to locate the most recent version of a document. Just pull down the View menu and choose By Date to see your files and folders listed with the most recently modified at the top.

daughterboard A small circuit board that plugs into a larger *motherboard*. Cute, huh? As far as I know, nobody has yet come up with a granddaughterboard, but it's bound to happen sooner or later. You just can't stop progress!

debug To find and fix programming errors, or bugs. Virtually all computer programs have bugs; it's just a fact of life that errors are going to creep in when you have something as complex as a typical program containing tens of thousands of lines of programming *code*. Software publishers try hard (some harder than others) to eliminate as many bugs as they can before shipping a product, but sooner or later some user tries something the program's *beta testers* didn't think of trying, and turns up an unexpected result—a bug. Responsible companies welcome bug reports from users, do their best to correct the problems, then issue new versions of their programs.

This is one reason you should always send in the registration card as soon as you buy a piece of software; if you don't, the publisher can't tell you about new versions of the program, which may fix important problems.

DEC (DEK) Digital Equipment Corporation. Well-known maker of *mini*computers, like the popular VAX machines (known to DEC groupies as "VAXen"). Lately, DEC has been making a valiant effort to get people to call it "Digital," but everybody just goes on saying "DEC." DEC's president, Ken Olson, once said "There is no reason for any individual to have a computer in their [sic] home." It should come as no surprise, then, that DEC's belated attempts to get into the personal computer market have all failed disastrously. Their minis, however, continue to be widely used.

decimal tab   A tab character used to make columns of numbers (like dollars-and-cents values) line up vertically on their decimal points at the tab's location.

$9.95
$.79
$10.74

default   What a program does if you don't tell it to do something else. For example, in most programs a new document will use the Geneva-12 font unless you specifically tell the program otherwise by choosing another font. We would describe this by saying that the program "defaults to" Geneva-12, or that Geneva-12 is the default font.

Another example: if you pull down the File menu and choose Page Setup, the dialog box that appears will have a number of options already checked. For *LaserWriter* users, these include things like *Font Substitution* and Text Smoothing. These are the defaults; unless you change them, your document will automatically be printed with these choices made for you.

delimiter   Any character used to separate items of information. For example, in the list "Monday,Tuesday,Wednesday" the delimiters are commas. Commas and tabs are the most frequently used delimiters.

density   The amount of data recorded on a *floppy disk*. Floppies come in three flavors: 1) Single density: 400K single-sided—an obsolete format; you're not likely to see these nowadays. 2) Double density: 800K double-sided; they look the same as the 400s. 3) High density: 1.44 MB double-sided; these can be distinguished from 400K and 800K disks by their extra rectangular hole (looking like a second *write-protect* hole, but with no sliding tab).

A word to the wise—if anybody ever tries to sell you a punch that will supposedly convert 800K disks to high-density disks by adding that extra hole, don't fall for it! The 1.44 MB high-density disks have a very different, higher-strength magnetic coating. While you might get away with using an 800K disk at 1.44 MB for a month or so, sooner or later it's apt to start forgetting your files. Remember: floppies are cheap compared to what your time is worth. So don't be tempted by the slick sales pitch. Just smile and walk away.

DES Data Encryption Standard. A widely used way of encoding information so that only its intended recipient can read it, it's often used with confidential financial records. Based on a US government standard, DES is supposed to be legal for use only in the US.

descender The part of a lowercase letter (like "p" or "j") that sticks down below the bases of the normal lowercase letters.

desk accessory A special type of mini-program, often abbreviated DA. Desk accessories used to be installed into your *System* with the dreaded *Font/DA Mover* program. Under *System 7*, there's no difference between a DA and any ordinary program. Whatever you put into the *Apple Menu Items* folder will show up on the *Apple menu*.

desktop 1) What you see when you start up your Mac, with the windows showing your disks' contents, the familiar *Trash*, and so on. The desktop display is created by the *Finder* as a visual metaphor to help you find, copy, delete, or open your files.

2) An invisible *directory* file called Desktop, found on each disk (hard or floppy), which catalogs the contents of that disk; it's used by the Finder to keep track of what's where. If the Desktop file has been damaged, either by a program that bombed or for other reasons, you may get the message "This disk needs minor repairs" or even "This disk is unreadable" when you try to use the disk. Programs like

Disk First Aid (which comes with your Mac) or the Norton Utilities (which you have to buy) can rebuild a damaged Desktop file if all else fails.

3) A word that Apple's marketing department applies wherever they hope it will help sell goods, as in Desktop Publishing, Desktop Video, Desktop Presentations, Desktop Media, Desktop Mapping, and so on.

developer A clever person who creates new software or hardware for your Mac. Developers are constantly struggling with Apple over who's to blame when software doesn't work. Apple says developers don't follow the rules when writing programs; developers counter that Apple often doesn't follow its own rules. Unfortunately, both sides are right. What happens when a developer doesn't follow the rules? See *bomb* or *crash*.

dialog box A message in a rectangular box that pops up on screen to ask you for more information.

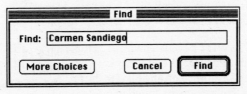

For example, when you choose the "Print..." command, a dialog asks how many copies you want, which pages to print, and so on. A dialog always appears when you choose a menu command followed by ellipses (...) like "Print..." or "Save As...". (Choosing a menu command without ellipses, like "Save", results in immediate action.)

digital Information or signals that change in discrete steps and can easily be translated to numbers (usually *binary* numbers); as opposed to *analog* signals, which change continuously.

digitize To convert an image or sound from *analog* (real world) to *digital* (computer) form in order to use it on the

Mac. It takes hardware to do this: for sounds, the audio input port on recent Macs will do; for images, a *scanner* or video camera is the usual method.

dimmed "Grayed out." In the case of menus, this means that the command in question is not available. When a disk icon is dimmed, it means that disk is already open.

DIN (DIN) Deutsche Industrie Norm. A large collection of German industrial standards; when Mac users throw this term around, they're referring to the particular round 8-pin connector used for printer and *modem* hookups on all recent Macs—a connector defined by one of the DIN standards.

dingbats A printer's term for an assortment of symbols such as arrows, stars, and fists. The *PostScript* typeface Zapf Dingbats (designed by the famous German typographer Hermann Zapf, in case you were wondering) is built into all PostScript LaserWriters except the discontinued LaserWriter Plus. Examples: ➔ ✍ ❏ ☞ ✂ ✈ ✪ ⇨ ❞

DIP switch (DIP SWITCH) Dual Inline Package. A row of tiny switches (usually turned on and off with the tip of a ballpoint pen), found in printers, *modems*, and other devices. They're used to set obscure things like start and *stop bits*, and are changed only when moving a device from one computer to another. This is a good thing, because the switches are usually unlabeled (other than by number) and figuring them out requires diligent reading of the user manual and a fair amount of profanity when the first few settings you try fail to work. (Remember, for eight switches there's one correct combination and 255 wrong ones!) This is one of the twentieth century's lousier ideas.

directory An area on a disk in which the Macintosh maintains a list of every file on that disk, where each file is physically located (which tracks and sectors), what type of file it is, and so on. It's roughly equivalent to the table of contents in a book. This file is invisible so that the uninitiated will be unable to delete or edit it.

A damaged directory is by far the most common cause of unreadable disks. If the directory is damaged (through either software malfunction or physical trauma such as leaving your disk near a magnet), the Finder doesn't know how to find anything on the disk and displays the message "This disk is unreadable" when you try to use it. (If the damage is slight, you may see "This disk needs minor repairs.") Fortunately, there are programs that can search the disk, find every file, and reconstruct the directory. Imagine trying to find chapters in a book with the table of contents torn out. You'd page through, note where each chapter starts, and reconstruct the missing table of contents chapter by chapter. Apple gives you one such program, Disk First Aid, but it isn't always smart enough to do the job; the commercial Norton Utilities has a far higher success rate.

directory dialog Apple's name for the *dialog* box you see when you ask a program to open a file or save one under a new name ("Save as..."). It lets you search your disk's *directory* to find a particular file or folder.

disabled When said of a control or a menu command, indicates that it's not presently available. Usually this is shown

by *dimming* or graying out the item. For example, if the Trash is already empty, the Finder command "Empty Trash" will be disabled.

disclaimer The fine print where the vendor tells you that you're on your own and that they guarantee absolutely nothing. For example: "Apple makes no warranty...with respect to software, its quality, performance, merchantability or fitness for a particular purpose. As a result, this software is sold 'as is,' and you the purchaser are assuming the entire risk as to its quality and performance." It's so reassuring when a company stands behind its products, isn't it? (That quotation was from the Macintosh System 6 User's Guide, by the way.)

Disinfectant Best of the public domain *virus*
protection programs, this is as good as any of
the commercial ones—and it's free! Unless you
choose to buy a program like S.A.M., you
should have this on your startup disk to protect against
virus infections, which can cause weird behavior, unexpected crashes, and worse. Because new viruses are
popping up all the time, it's important to have the latest
version of Disinfectant. Available free from *information
services* like *AOL* and *CompuServe* and from user groups.

disk In computer lingo, a thin plastic or metal disk coated
with a film of material that can be selectively magnetized
in order to store computer data. It's the same principle as
a tape recorder, but a computer disk works much faster.
Disks come in two varieties: *hard disks* and *floppy disks*.

Disk Cache See *cache*.

disk drive A device analogous to a tape recorder, it uses
a magnetic disk to record and play back computer information such as programs and documents. *Hard disk*
drives contain a permanently mounted disk; with *floppy*
drives, you must insert a floppy disk to record data and
remove it when you're done.

diskette See *floppy disk*.

dither To simulate colors or grays using a mixture of dots.
For example, some older graphics programs could display
a given *pixel*, or screen dot, in one of eight colors, and
purple wasn't one of them. However, by creating a check-
erboard pattern of alternating red and blue, they could
simulate purple (if you didn't look too closely).

Dithering relies on the eye's tendency to blend
fine patterns together, a fact well known to the
pointillist painters of the last century. In the
same way, displays and printers that can't create
varying levels of gray (true of all except *dye-sublimation*
printers) can simulate gray by using patterns of black dots,
as in the example shown; this is more commonly known as
halftoning in the printing trade.

D

Dithering involves a trade-off: the more different colors or levels of gray you want to simulate, the lower your usable resolution, or sharpness—because it takes a whole cluster of black-and-white dots to simulate each gray pixel. Thus, a 300-dot-per-inch (dpi) *LaserWriter* printing a dithered photograph with 32 simulated gray levels has an effective resolution of only about 55 dpi. There ain't no such thing as a free lunch—as the number of gray levels goes up, resolution goes down.

document A disk file, usually consisting mostly of data, created by an application such as MacWrite or Excel. Business letters, *HyperCard stacks*, and MacPaint pictures are all Macintosh documents.

dogcow The beloved mascot of Apple's Developer Technical Services, this mythical animal can be seen in the Options part of the Print dialog. And what does a dogcow say? Why, "Moof!", of course.

dongle A small, individually serial-numbered device—a sort of electronic key—that plugs into a *serial, SCSI,* or *ADB port,* this is a particularly obnoxious form of hardware *copy protection.* When the copy-protected program runs, it checks to see that the dongle is there and has the correct serial number. That sounds fine in theory, but in practice almost always results in pesky compatibility problems with other manufacturers' software and hardware. Mercifully, this scheme is rare nowadays.

DOS (DOSS) Disk Operating System. In common usage, short for *MS-DOS.*

dot matrix printer A widely misused term; in reality, all printers (except the obsolete daisywheel types) fit this definition, since they all create their images from tiny dots. However, it's commonly used to refer to impact dot matrix printers, which create characters and graphics by physically slamming small pins against the ribbon and paper, thereby causing black dots to appear.

download 1) To receive a file (for example, an *electronic mail* message or a computer program) from another computer or computer *network,* like *AOL, CompuServe,* or a private *BBS.* This is usually done by using a *modem* to communicate with the other computer over the phone. Many excellent programs can be downloaded very cheaply from networks like AOL.

2) To send a *PostScript* font from your Mac to a *LaserWriter* or similar printer in order to use a typeface that isn't built into the LaserWriter.

downloadable font A *PostScript* font sent from your Mac to a *LaserWriter* or similar printer in order to use a typeface that isn't already built into the LaserWriter. Also called a *printer font* or *outline font.*

dpi dots per inch. A measure of printer or screen resolution. For example, the standard Mac screen displays 72 dpi; a *LaserWriter* printer can print 300 dpi.

drag To push and hold down the mouse button while moving the mouse; this is how you move a document to the Trash, for example.

drag and drop 1) A concept introduced by System 7; this means to drag a file's icon on top of another file's icon and release it, causing some action to occur. For example, if you drag a MacWrite document's icon and drop it onto the MacWrite program's icon, the program will be run and the document opened.

2) Microsoft uses this phrase in a completely different way, to mean selecting and moving data without cutting and pasting.

DRAM (DEE ʀᴀᴍ) Dynamic Random Access Memory. A widely used type of semiconductor memory (see *RAM)* that's inexpensive but consumes more power than its more expensive cousin, static RAM (SRAM). It's called "dynamic" because, like the French you learned in high school, it must be constantly exercised or the contents are quickly forgotten. (An in-between type, pseudostatic RAM, exercises itself automatically; it uses less power than DRAM but more than SRAM.)

draw program A graphics program that uses *object-oriented* or *vector graphics* (as opposed to *bitmapped* graphics). MacDraw was the original such program on the Macintosh; most graphics programs now include at least some draw-type features.

driver A small piece of software needed to use a hardware accessory such as a printer, scanner, or hard disk. Drivers usually live in the *System Folder*; the most common are printer drivers such as *LaserWriter* and ImageWriter.

DTP DeskTop Publishing. Really a misnomer, this means desktop *typesetting*, since the printing is almost always done elsewhere. DTP uses computers, programs like Page-Maker, and high-quality printers like the LaserWriter to produce *camera-ready copy*.

dumb quotes The kind used by dumb people, natch—typewriter quotes ("), which really should only be used as inch marks or in programming. Smart people use *smart quotes* (by pressing the Option key and [or]) whenever they can.

dumping When an American company introduces a product at a low price in order to penetrate an established market, that's called smart marketing. When a Japanese company does this, it's called dumping, and we retaliate with trade sanctions, quotas, and big import surcharges.

DVI Digital Video Interactive. A system proposed by Intel that puts computer programs, text, graphics, and highly compressed video onto a *CD-ROM*. It's intended to be used for training and reference purposes. Similar to Phillips' *CD-I*, but not aimed at consumers.

DXF Data eXchange Format. The file format of documents created by AutoCAD, a *DOS* program with perhaps the ugliest *user interface* in history. DXF is an industry standard (even in the Mac industry!) for *CAD* files.

dye-sublimation A printer technology, presently very expensive, that can put ink in varying colors and densities on the paper, thus eliminating the need for *dithering* to obtain delicate tints and shades. The result is a high-resolution, true-color printout that looks very much like a color photograph. By comparison, most color printers yield output that looks like a coarse newspaper photo. Someday dye-sub printers will be affordable, I hope! In the meantime, if this book sells really well....

Ee

Easy Access A *control panel* provided by Apple to help make Macs usable for people who have trouble typing with two hands or using a mouse. Easy Access lets you use the numeric keypad instead of the mouse to move the *pointer;* type two-key commands (like Command-C) with just one finger; and it can make the keyboard wait awhile before accepting a keystroke—very useful if you're an uncertain typist. If you like audible feedback while you type, Easy Access can also generate key-click noises.

edition A file that contains the part of a document that was *published,* a special function of System 7. When you make changes to the master document (the edition's publisher), you can choose to have the edition file automatically updated. Other documents can *subscribe* to the edition and include its contents, which can be automatically updated when the edition changes. This publish-and-subscribe mechanism is System 7's way of providing a link between documents from different programs—sort of like an automated form of cutting and pasting.

eject tool A straightened paper clip used as a last-resort tool to eject a stuck *floppy disk.* You should very rarely have to do this, but if a defective disk (or one with a label that's loose or peeling off) becomes stuck in your drive, you can remove it by inserting the straightened end of a paper clip into the little hole just to the right of the disk slot. Use a heavy-duty paper clip so it won't buckle, and be sure to push it straight in. Why didn't Apple give us a disk-eject button like the ones on *DOS* machines? Because manually ejecting a floppy without giving the Mac a chance to update its *Desktop (directory)* file can leave you with an unreadable disk. So, only use this trick in a real emergency—and never, ever use Post-it™ notes as disk labels!

electronic mail A message or file sent to another user of a computer bulletin board system *(BBS)* or *network*. Usually called *email*.

ELF Extremely Low Frequency. Refers to both electromagnetic and electrostatic fields given off by most electric motors and by computer monitors. Some evidence (still controversial) suggests that ELF radiation from computer monitors can be a health hazard. While final proof is still lacking, it's probably wise to play it safe and not sit too close to that color monitor on your desk. Some companies sell special faceplate shields for your *CRT* and claim that they'll reduce or eliminate all dangerous radiations. Don't be fooled; they don't work for ELF. A word of advice: if you notice that your fingernails are starting to glow in the dark, you probably should cut back your computer usage!

ellipsis Three widely spaced periods (…) used to indicate that material has been omitted from a quotation. For example, a reviewer panning a recent show described it as "The kind of musical that is—fortunately—seldom seen on Broadway nowadays." The show's producers ran large ads quoting the review: "THE KIND OF MUSICAL...SELDOM SEEN ON BROADWAY NOWA-DAYS!" That's what you can do with three little dots and a complete lack of scruples. Of course, you can always just type three periods...but to get properly spaced ellipses, hold down the Option key and press semicolon (;).

email (EE MAIL) Abbreviation for *electronic mail*.

em dash A longer than normal dash, like this—in fact, it's exactly as long as the lowercase letter "m"—often used to separate clauses in a sentence. Remember how your typing teacher taught you to use two hyphens for this purpose? Well, forget that amateur stuff—use an em dash instead! To get one, hold down the Shift and Option keys and press hyphen.

emulation Imitation, as in, "This program emulates a DEC VT-100 video terminal." Usually, as in this example, emulation means software imitating hardware.

encrypt To scramble the contents of a file so that nobody can decipher it except the person who has a special software "key." You can do this to prevent prying people from peeping at your private projects (say that three times fast!), personnel files, love letters, or your Super Secret Master Plan for conquering the universe.

en dash A slightly longer than normal dash—in fact, it's exactly as long as the lowercase letter "n"—used to separate telephone numbers or ranges of values, as in, "To use System 7 effectively, you need 4–8 MB of memory." To get an en dash, hold down the Option key and press hyphen.

endless loop See *infinite loop*.

engine Usually seen in references to scanners and laser printers, this is the mechanical guts—the gears and stuff—that make something work. For example, "The Apple Personal LaserWriters use a Canon LX engine" means that Apple buys the mechanical/optical/electrical printer parts like the paper transport, laser assembly, and power supply from Canon, then adds its own controller board (the "brains" of the printer) plus, of course, an Apple-designed outer case.

enterprise A fancy word for "business," used in buzz phrases like "enterprise computing" to project the image of something more important, advanced, and modern than plain old "business." It's equivalent to calling an undertaker a "grief counselor."

EOF End Of File. Usually a special character written after the data portion of a disk file; when the file is being read in from the disk and the program encounters an EOF, it knows that's all there is and it can stop reading. If you ever get the error message "Unexpected EOF encountered" while trying to open a document, it probably means the file has been damaged on the disk.

EPS (or **EPSF**) Encapsulated PostScript (Format). A way of storing a PostScript graphic image so that it can be conveniently placed into a document thereby allowing the user to see a low-resolution on-screen approximation of the image's final appearance.

Why add the low-res preview? Because a PostScript graphic is not a picture in the ordinary sense; it's actually a program in the PostScript language, and it takes a PostScript interpreter to display or print it. (See *PostScript* for more on how this works.) The PostScript interpreter is very large and complex, and the vast majority of Mac programs don't have one. For that reason, if you place an ordinary (non-EPS) PostScript graphic into, say, a PageMaker document, all PageMaker can show you is a gray box the size of the picture.

This is not very satisfying, so Aldus, Altsys, and Adobe came up with the idea of adding a bitmapped image (for screen viewing only) to the PostScript graphic. The two images are encapsulated into one file, hence the name Encapsulated PostScript. When you view an EPS graphic on

PostScript   PICT bitmap

the screen, you're really looking at a 72-dpi *PICT* bitmap— something any program can display without needing special interpreters. It's a low-resolution image, but good enough to let you see what you're working with on the screen. When you send the document to a PostScript printer (like a LaserWriter), the PICT is ignored and the PostScript part is printed out in all its high-resolution glory.

ergonomics The science of making tools comfortably usable by humans. Does that sound simple? Well, it's subtler and more complicated than you might imagine. For example, the original Apple][keyboard had a *reset* key located right next to the return key. Unfortunately, it was all too easy to accidentally reset the computer and lose all your work! Bad ergonomic design.

The original Macs had a reset switch protruding from the left side of the case. This was a bit better, but if you accidentally pushed a book or other object up against the computer, you could still bump the switch and reset the Mac. Apple finally recognized the problem and redesigned the switch. With the SE and later machines it's set flush and can't be accidentally pushed. Little things like that make a big difference!

Ergonomics also affects things like the way your furniture is designed, and the lamp on your desk. For example, the popular new halogen lamps cast a harsh, contrasty light; ergonomic studies show this is more tiring for your eyes than soft, diffuse illumination. You may not consciously notice poor ergonomic design, but if you find yourself tiring easily and suffering unexplained aches and pains, it may well be due to bad "human engineering"—poor ergonomics.

escape 1) A key on your keyboard ("esc"); some programs let you use it to interrupt an operation in progress. (This is more commonly done by holding down the *Command key* while pressing period.)

2) An *ASCII* character (decimal value 27) that is generated when you press the esc key.

Ethernet A high-speed *networking* standard developed by Xerox in the sixties and now available for Macintoshes. Although more expensive than *AppleTalk,* it's about ten times faster. Computers on an Ethernet network can be connected by thick or thin *coaxial cable* or by *twisted pair (10BaseT)* wiring; these three wiring schemes are mutually incompatible.

EtherTalk Software from Apple that lets you connect up an *AppleTalk network* using *Ethernet* cables so that your Macs can talk to each other at Ethernet speeds using the familiar AppleTalk interface.

expand To reveal the lower levels of an outline view; the opposite of *collapse.* In Mac usage:

1) In a text-view Finder window, to show the contents of a folder by clicking on the triangle to the left of its name.

2) To display an outline document with its subheadings showing.

extended   A horizontally stretched typeface. Opposite of *condensed*.

extension   A bit of software that adds functionality to your Mac's *operating system*. Extensions (which used to be called *INITs* or *cdevs*) are automatically loaded

Network Extension

when your Mac starts up, and they add features ranging from *screen savers* like Pyro to the animation capabilities of *QuickTime*. Extensions like *MODE32* patch your system in order to correct bugs. Under System 7, extensions can be found in the Extensions folder inside your System Folder.

Extensions   A special folder inside your *System Folder*. Under System 7, *extensions* must be placed in this folder in order to work properly.

Ff

FatBits An eight-power blowup of a screen *bitmap*. The term was coined by Bill *Atkinson* to describe the magnification feature in the original 1984 MacPaint program, which was activated by holding down the *Command* *key* while clicking with the Pencil tool. Almost all bitmapped graphics programs written since then include the same shortcut—it's a Mac tradition.

fax Short for "facsimile" (Latin for "make a likeness"); a simple way of creating an electronic equivalent of a paper document (for example, a business contract), sending it over the phone lines and recreating a paper version on the other end. The device used to do this is basically a combined *scanner, modem,* and medium-resolution (200 dots per inch) printer. You can use a separate, self-contained fax machine, or if you already have a Mac with a scanner and a good printer, you can buy a fax modem, which uses your Mac and its accessories to do the same job. In either case the transmitted file is a giant *bitmap,* readable by human eyes but unintelligible to a word processor.

FDHD Floppy Disk/High Density (also known as SuperFloppy). A floppy disk drive in current Macs that reads and writes 400K, 800K, and high-*density* 1.4 megabyte disks. With the proper software, it can understand not only Mac disks but *Apple][* ProDOS disks and *MS-DOS* disks from the newer IBM computers and *clones*.

fiber optics A way of transmitting information with light instead of electricity, using thin glass or plastic fibers instead of wires. Because light waves can carry much more information than can electrical signals, fiber-optic cables are good for video or high-speed computer data, which strain the capacity of copper wires. Fiber optics also have the advantage of being immune to interference from

F

other sources. By contrast, electrical cables act as minia-
ture antennas, both radiating and picking up spurious
signals that can garble information.

field 1) Half of a television picture. In the *NTSC* television
system used in the US, each *frame* of the image is composed of 525 horizontal scan lines. Rather than transmit
the whole frame at once, it's sent as two fields, each of
which has 262.5 lines: first the odd-numbered lines are
transmitted, then the even-numbered ones. The two fields
interlace on the picture tube: every other scan line belongs
to a different field; hence this system is called "interlaced
video."

Why this seemingly complicated scheme? Because it
prevents annoying flicker by sending part of a picture sixty
times a second instead of a whole picture thirty times a
second, and does so without requiring more expensive
high-*bandwidth* circuits. Newer systems (like the Mac's
video displays) show the whole frame sixty to seventy
times a second, yielding higher resolution with no flicker.
This is called "noninterlaced video."

2) A piece of information, like a name or phone number,
in a *database;* part of a data *record*. Think of a record as
being equivalent to a 3" x 5" file card, and the fields as
being like the lines of information on the card.

file A program or document that appears on your
desktop in the form of an icon with a filename
under it. If it isn't a folder (which holds a collection of files) and you can copy it from one disk to
another, it's a file.

file creator See *creator*.

file sharing Apple's way of letting you use the files on
another Mac. The two machines must be connected by a
network and have System 7 installed. (The network can be
as simple as two Macs sharing a printer via *AppleTalk.)*
Shared files and folders appear on your desktop and you
can work with them just as though they were on your own
hard disk.

film recorder An output device that creates on film a high-resolution color image of a document. Most film recorders can display many more dots than a standard 640 x 480 Mac color screen (usually at least 2000 x 1500), yielding a much sharper picture than you could get by simply pointing a camera at the screen. They are mostly used to produce color 35mm slides for presentations and for publication.

Finder A program that lives in your *System Folder;* it creates the desktop-like environment you work with when you first start up or when you're copying files and disks. It puts the windows, icons, and Trash icon onto the screen, lets you drag them around, and moves disks and files as you tell it to. (It's called the "Finder" because it helps you find the files you want to work with.) The Finder is like a translator between you and the System: you drag an icon from one desktop window to another, and the Finder tells the System "Copy that file!" Then the System tells the disk drives to start up, reads the file from one disk, and writes it to another.

FinePrint A clever bit of software built into Apple's *LaserWriter* IIf and IIg printers, this makes type and line graphics look a bit sharper than normal. It does so by modulating the printer's laser beam at a high rate of speed, creating "fractional dots" that are used to increase the printer's apparent resolution above the normal 300 dots per inch.

firmware Software that's programmed into read-only memory chips *(ROMs)* so that it can't be changed. All computers (and most accessories like printers or plug-in *boards)* have firmware so that they'll know what to do when you turn them on.

FKEY (EFF KEE) Function KEY. (Not to be confused with the *function keys* on the Extended keyboard.) A small utility program that can be invoked by holding down the Shift and *Command keys* and typing a number. One example is the Shift-Command-3 FKEY built into your Mac, which causes a *PICT* file to be created with the contents of the screen. There are also many public domain FKEYs available. Technically, FKEYs are resources of type 'FKEY'.

FLA Four-Letter Acronym. Something you frequently run into in the computer business. You can just imagine the engineers sitting in their offices saying to themselves, "Hmmm...neat idea. Now all it needs is an FLA...how about 'SCSI'...or maybe 'TIFF'..." (Of course, "FLA" itself is a TLA—a Three-Letter Acronym.) Riddle: What's the difference between the computer industry and a truckload of Alpha Bits? Answer: The industry has more letters!

flame A strongly worded and often an- gry message posted on an electronic bulletin board *(BBS)*. The etiquette of BBS discussions is strikingly different from that of a face-to-face discussion. Many times a simple opinion, casually tossed off ("The Apple][is pitifully outdated—it should've been discontinued years ago") can provoke an unexpectedly heated response, or flame. This in turn leads to a counter-response until a full-fledged "flame war" erupts, with many users taking turns in shouting out their opinions and tearing down each other's arguments (and, eventually, characters). Flame wars can be pretty vicious, but tend to peter out eventually, with the participants limping off to lick their wounds in private.

flat-file A *database* that can't be cross-indexed to another; as opposed to a *relational* database. Flat-file database programs such as FileMaker are less complex and less expensive than relational database managers such as 4th Dimension.

floating point In mathematical terms, this describes a "real" number—one that has a fractional or decimal part—as opposed to a whole number or integer. It's called a floating point number because it has a decimal point that "floats," depending on the number's size. On the Mac, floating point calculations are done by the system's *SANE* number-crunching routines, sometimes with help from a numeric *coprocessor chip*.

floppy disk A small, flat object about 3.5" square that stores files used by your Macintosh. Inside the hard plastic case is a small, thin disk of flexible plastic material very similar to the tape in a videocassette; the Mac's *disk drive* spins this around like a record, while a *read/write head* similar to that in a tape recorder records and plays back data on the disk, which is coated with magnetic oxide. Floppies are inexpensive, but they hold only limited amounts of information (1.44 megabytes is pretty much standard) and are slow compared to hard disks.

F

floptical A "floppy optical" (actually *magneto-optical)* disk.

flow chart A standard way of diagramming any step-by-step procedure, including a computer program. Basically, you break the process down into steps, write each step inside a little box, and connect the boxes with arrows. Special symbols are often used to show decision points, 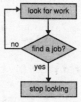 inputs, and outputs. Because a flow chart shows which steps depend on which other steps, it's useful for analyzing a task's sequence.

folder A place to keep related programs or documents together. Folders can contain other folders, so you could create a folder called "Taxes" and have within it folders called "1990," "1991," and "1992". If you're used to *MS-DOS*, a folder is equivalent to a DOS subdirectory.

font A specific set of character shapes that make up all the letters, numbers, and symbols of a typeface. For example, Geneva, Times, Courier, and Zapf Chancery are fonts, in Apple's parlance. There are three kinds of fonts: screen or *bitmap* fonts, *PostScript* fonts, and *TrueType* fonts. Bitmap fonts come in fixed sizes and are really useful only for screen display. They generally print poorly and cannot be resized.

a
bitmapped

a
PostScript

PostScript fonts are mathematical descriptions of character shapes. They can be printed any size at all and will look as good as your printer can make them look. (The more dots per inch, the better the result. The range is from 300 dots per inch in the case of the PostScript *LaserWriters*, up to 2540 dpi with the PostScript-compatible Linotronic *imagesetters*.) Apple's TrueType fonts are sort of a low-rent version of PostScript fonts; they share the advantages of printer independence, but are less flexible in what they can do in the way of special effects.

Font/DA Mover A utility program supplied by Apple, it was previously required in order to install *fonts* and *desk accessories* into your *System* file. Since most people found it confusing (I always liked it myself), Apple made it unnecessary. With System 7, you just drag the fonts to the *System Folder* and the *Finder* knows where to put them.

font ID (FONT I DEE) Every Macintosh *font* has an ID number that identifies it to the Mac's *operating system* and the programs that use it. Trouble is, there are now so many thousands of fonts that you often find several fonts using the same ID! *Font/DA Mover* renumbers fonts to prevent such conflicts, but that just makes things more confusing for programs. Well-behaved Mac programs nowadays refer to fonts by name, not by number, which helps reduce the problem of your office memo showing up in *dingbats* when you open it on a different Mac.

Font Substitution An option in the Page Setup dialog box, this automatically substitutes *PostScript* fonts for certain bitmapped fonts when you print your document. Specifically, Geneva turns into Helvetica, New York turns into Times, and Monaco (ugh!) turns into Courier (double ugh!).

This sounds like a handy feature, but you should avoid it like the plague. Why? The three bitmapped fonts are much wider than their PostScript cousins; after substitution, you end up with a lot of space between the words (as in these two lines) in your printout. The result looks terrible, and it's a dead giveaway of an amateur. So remember: turn off font substitution, stay away from fonts with city names (like these three), and always use PostScript fonts when printing to a laser printer!

footer Text (or sometimes graphics) that appears at the bottom of each page of a multipage document. For example, the footer for this dictionary has only a page number in it.

footprint The amount of space a piece of equipment takes up on your desk. Some external *hard disk* drives are called "zero footprint" devices because you can stack a Mac SE or Classic on top of the drive and not use up any more space than the computer alone uses.

fork Any Macintosh file (a program or document) can have two parts: a data fork and/or a resource fork. You won't see them as separate parts unless you use a utility program like *ResEdit*, but the Macintosh's operating system knows they're there. Not all files have both parts. Programs always have resources and may also have data; documents always have data and may also have resources.

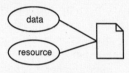

format 1) To erase a disk (either hard or floppy) completely and prepare it for new data. (Apple calls this "initializing.") Don't do this unless you're really sure you want to wipe everything off the disk!

2) The characteristics of a piece of text: for example, its *font*, size, style, and *leading*.

formatter A special utility program used to completely erase a *hard disk*. Most formatters can also do useful things like testing a disk, rewriting its *boot blocks*, and *partitioning* it.

form generator A program specially designed to help you create forms—documents intended to elicit information from someone in an organized, standardized way. The forms can be either printed out on paper or saved as computer-based forms that can be filled in *online*.

Fortran FORmula TRANslator. An extremely ancient, almost prehistoric (fifties vintage) computer language. It's still used for scientific and engineering tasks—not because it's a good language, but because there's so much Fortran *code* already written that it's often easier to simply crib what you need than to write it yourself.

FPU Floating Point Unit. A *coprocessor chip* specialized for numerical calculations. It works in tandem with your regular *microprocessor* to speed up operations that require heavy number-crunching.

fragmentation 1) A condition in which a disk (usually a *hard disk*) has its stored *files* broken up into small fragments, resulting in slow operation. Information is stored on a disk in concentric *tracks,* each of which is divided into a number of *sectors.* When a disk is new, files are written one after another, to *contiguous* sectors. As you add, delete, and change your documents, the *operating system* does its best to use all the available space on the disk. For example, if you delete a document near the beginning of the disk, then copy a longer file onto the disk, the system uses the sectors left by the deleted file to store as much of the new file as will fit, then puts the rest of the new file into the first available open space. This means that the new file is now in two parts on the disk—it's fragmented.

Although this isn't a problem for the operating system (which knows where to find both parts), it means that instead of reading the whole file off the disk in one fell swoop, the system has to read one part, move the drive's *read/write head* to somewhere else, then read the second part. This takes a little longer. After you've been using your Mac for a few months, you end up with files in many pieces scattered all over the disk, and you may find that loading a file takes noticeably longer than it used to. Your disk has become fragmented.

There are two things you can do to remedy the situation: either use a commercial defragmenting program like Norton's Speed Disk, or do a complete backup, then copy all the files back to your disk. Either way, you'll end up with each file stored in contiguous sectors so that the drive's head needs a minimum of back-and-forth movement to read or write the file.

2) A condition analogous to disk fragmentation that can occur in a computer's *RAM* (memory) when several programs have occupied chunks of memory. The remedy is to quit your programs and restart them—or, in extreme cases, restart the Mac altogether.

frame A single, still video or film image; $1/30$ of a second worth of frozen reality ($1/24$, in the case of movies on film).

frame grabber A piece of hardware that in $1/30$ of a second (the duration of a single video *frame)* can convert that frame into a computer-based *bitmap* image. This is a way of getting images from a video camera, VCR, or videodisc player into the Mac, where you can play with them using graphics programs like Photoshop. Most frame grabbers are *NuBus* boards for use in Mac II series computers.

freeze A type of *crash* in which a program is locked up and becomes unresponsive to keystrokes or mouse clicks—in a word, goes catatonic. In severe cases, the *cursor* may even freeze in place on the screen. The remedy is usually to *reset* your Mac, but doing so often means losing data.

Frontier A system from a company called UserLand that lets you control your applications (including the Finder) by writing *scripts* (small programs) in a language called UserTalk. For example, you can write a script that does the following: at midnight (when phone rates are low), it logs onto America Online, gets the latest scores in the Intercollegiate Quilting Championships, logs off, pastes the numbers into an Excel spreadsheet, plots a graph comparing the scores by geographical region, copies it to the Clipboard, starts up PageMaker, opens your quilting club's newsletter, pastes in the graph, and prints the document. (Whew!) All this without your being anywhere near the computer. You get the idea: these are very powerful capabilities—if you can figure out how to write the scripts. One other catch: Frontier uses *AppleEvents* to tell programs what to do, and not all programs understand AppleEvents yet. But *real soon now (RSN)*…

full duplex A type of computer-to-computer hookup (usually via telephone lines) in which each character you type on your keyboard is sent to the other computer, which in turn echoes it back to your screen for display. It's the opposite of *half duplex,* in which the other computer does not echo back your transmissions, and the transmissions must be directly displayed by your own computer.

There are no big advantages either way, and both systems are used; however, if you have your computer set to the wrong mode when trying to communicate with another computer, you're going to get strange results. For example, if you type "HELLO" and see "HHEELLOO" on your screen, you're in half duplex and the other computer's in full duplex. If you see nothing when you type, you may be in full duplex and the other machine in half duplex.

function key 1) A key at the top of the Apple Extended Keyboard (F1 through F15) used by some programs to activate special functions.

2) A software utility invoked by pressing Shift, *Command,* and a number key; see *FKEY.*

fuser The part of a *LaserWriter* that applies heat and pressure to a printout in order to permanently fuse its black *toner* image to the paper.

fx fast, expensive [Mac]. See *Macintosh.*

Gg

Gates, Bill Very smart, very determined, and very, very rich, Bill Gates is one of the most powerful figures in the computer industry. Back in 1975 when Bill was just a cocky kid, he and his friend Paul Allen were hired to write a version of the *BASIC* language for the Altair microcomputer kit—as it turned out, a better BASIC than the original. Calling their company *Microsoft,* they rapidly built their BASIC into a highly profitable industry standard (much to the disgust of BASIC's inventors, Dartmouth's Kemeny and Kurtz).

Gates' big break came in 1980 when IBM came knocking on the door, looking for a disk operating system for the new IBM *PC.* Microsoft didn't have one, but they were able to buy a system called "Quick and Dirty DOS" from a couple of local hackers. Renamed "*MS-DOS,*" it rode on the PC's coattails to become another industry standard.

Gates and Microsoft (the two are hard to separate!) now dominate the PC side of the personal computer industry, and Microsoft's Excel and Word programs are also best sellers on the Mac. Bill Gates has very definite ideas of what road the industry should be on, and Microsoft has been a very effective steamroller for paving that road—to the dismay of some who got in the way.

gateway A device or program that connects two different kinds of computer *networks* and translates between their *protocols,* or ways of sending information.

Geneva A *sans serif bitmapped* font designed by Susan *Kare* in 1983. It was loosely patterned after the well-known commercial font Helvetica. (You Latin scholars out there will recognize that "Helvetia" was the Roman name for Switzerland, of which Geneva is the capital.) Geneva was specifically designed for readability on the Mac's low-resolution, 72-dpi screen. Although you can print it out on paper—and Apple even provides a

TrueType version nowadays—Geneva looks awkward coming from a 300-dpi LaserWriter; its proportions are too wide and its character shapes too exaggerated for use in print. So keep Geneva for screen use, but if you're planning to print something out, use Helvetica instead—that's what it was designed for.

GEnie (GEE NEE) A large computer *network* with hundreds of thousands of subscribers. You can call GEnie with your computer and a *modem* connected to your phone line; for an hourly fee, you can download programs, read the news from various wire services, track your investments, shop, send mail, ask for help with computer problems, and a lot more. Other commercial *information services* include the Mac like *AOL* and the larger and more expensive *CompuServe*.

genlock To synchronize two video signals perfectly so that they can be mixed. A video signal has a distinctive rhythm—much too fast for you to hear, of course, but the beat is always there, line by line, frame by frame. In a TV studio, all the cameras, videotape recorders and special effects generators march in step, locked to the beat of a master sync generator—genlocked.

But home video and computer equipment is different. Each camcorder, VCR, or computer video board has its own sync generator, and these never quite match up with each other. That makes it impossible to mix signals, as you need to do if you want to overlay computer-generated titles on a videotape, or even just do a dissolve from one scene to another. To get around this problem, you use a genlock circuit to slave one device (usually the computer video board) to another, allowing the signals to be mixed cleanly—because they're both marching in step to the same beat.

Get Info... A useful command on the Finder's File menu that lets you find out things like how big a file is, when it was created and modified, what version it is (if it's a program), and what program created it (if it's a document).

GHz See *gigahertz*.

gigabyte (GIH GUH BITE) Roughly a billion *bytes*; that is, 1024 megabytes.

gigahertz Billions of cycles per second (one Hertz is one cps). Abbreviated *GHz*.

GIGO (GUY GO) Garbage In, Garbage Out. A favorite saying of programmers, who like to remind you that even a perfect program will give wrong answers if fed incorrect data—an all too common occurrence!

glitch A malfunction, usually caused by a hardware problem; a slipup. From German "glitschen," to slip.

global change A change that's made throughout a document. All word processors can do this automatically for you. For example, you might change all occurrences of "degrees" to "°", or all occurrences of "Richard M. Nixon" to "Tricky Dicky."

glossary A useful feature of some word processors, this lets you type an abbreviation like "AARP" and have the program automatically fill in "AppleTalk Address Resolution Protocol." Or "American Association of Retired Persons"—it's up to you. A great time saver, especially for slow typists like me!

Gouraud shading (GOO ROW) A way of *rendering* (that is, depicting realistic shadows and reflections) a simulated 3D object in a CAD program; named after the French author of this rendering *algorithm*. Other methods include *Phong shading* and *radiosity*.

grabber The little hand icon with which you can move your document around in its window. First seen in the original MacPaint, the grabber has become a standard tool in most Mac graphics programs.

graphics smoothing A choice in the Page Setup dialog box, this works with Apple *LaserWriters* and some other printers to alleviate the jagged look of *bitmapped* graphics when they're printed. (It really should have been called "bitmap smoothing.") It helps, but if you can possibly use *object-oriented* graphics instead, you'll get a much better looking printout. You should also be aware that graphics smoothing slows down printing tremendously.

graphics tablet   An input device that lets you use a pen-like stylus instead of a mouse. Tablets are especially loved by artists, who are painfully aware that drawing with a mouse is like drawing with a bar of soap. The best graphics tablets, like the widely used *Wacom*, have pressure-sensitive styli that can work with software to create the illusion of a paintbrush, a marker pen, a charcoal stick, or anything you want.

grayscale   A range of gray tones from black to white, as displayed on a video screen or seen by a *scanner*. The amount of memory available for each *pixel*, or image dot, determines how many levels of gray (including black and white) can be represented. For example, 8 bits per pixel (as in Apple's scanner) permit 256 levels of gray to be represented (since $2^8 = 256$). Although it's common to speak of printing grays, most current Macintosh printers can print only solid black—not gray—dots. In order to simulate grays, it's necessary to resort to *dithering* or *halftoning*—the use of fine patterns of black and white dots that will fool the eye into seeing gray.

greek   To display very small text as gray bars instead of tiny individual letters. Why on earth would you want to do this? Well, in a *page layout program* you often need to zoom out and look at a whole document in order to rearrange things on the page. If you have a Mac Classic and you're trying to look at a two-page spread on your 9" screen, you aren't going to be able to read the text in your document anyway (because it'll be 1 pixel high!)—and the Mac will waste a lot of time trying to draw all those itty-bitty characters. So programs like PageMaker will automatically greek any text that's less than, say, 6 pixels high on the screen. You'll see gray areas that give you a general idea of where your text blocks are, and the Mac will be able to update your screen much faster. The text will still print normally, of course, and when you go back to 100% magnification you'll be able to read it again.

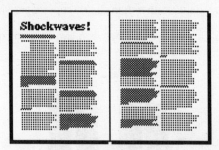

grid A mode found in most graphics programs and in the *Finder*. Like a lawn chair whose back angle adjusts in half-inch steps, the grid makes objects or drawing tools move in discrete intervals, making it easier to align things. When you drag an object and let go, it "snaps" to the nearest grid location. The Views *control panel* lets you turn on a grid for Finder icons, making it easy to keep your *desktop* looking neat.

group To fasten several graphics objects together so they can be moved and resized as a unit. Programs like *Illustrator* and MacDraw let you do this as a way of creating a "subassembly" which can then be manipulated as if it were a single object. All you have to do is select all the objects and issue the Group command, and they're locked together (until you Ungroup them again).

groupware Software that can be used by several people at once, assuming they're connected by a *network*. For example, a newspaper might have editors, writers, and staff artists all working on parts of the same document at the same time using groupware.

guest A person without a password on a computer *network* who is using the resources of another computer (a *server*).

GUI (GOO EE) Graphical User Interface. An acronym popular with *PC* users, it's applied to Mac lookalikes such as *Windows*. By coining this brand new buzz phrase for what Mac users have enjoyed since 1984, the *PC* crowd tries to maintain the fiction that they're really inventing great new stuff, rather than simply copying old Mac ideas.

gutter The white space between two columns of text or between two facing pages in a publication.

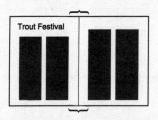

GWorld (GEE WORLD) Graphics World. When the Mac is working with a graphic image, the image is stored in memory along with its related data (like color *palettes*). This collection of data is called a GWorld. Normally stored in your Mac's main memory, the GWorld is repeatedly copied to *video RAM* (memory) as you work on the image so that you can see what you're doing.

But if you're working on a large 24-bit color image, all that copying back and forth can slow things down. That's why some video boards (such as Apple's 8•24 GC) have their own GWorld memory. The entire GWorld is stored right on the board, making it possible to quickly display any changes. This means better performance—a good thing, obviously. There's one catch: the program you're using has to know how to take advantage of GWorld RAM, and right now most do not. PageMaker, Photoshop, and PixelPaint Pro are among the few that do. If you have a video card with onboard GWorld RAM, these programs will run substantially faster.

Hh

hacker A programming enthu-  siast or dedicated hobbyist; someone who programs for the sheer fun of it. The word was first used in this sense in the early sixties by members of the Massachusetts Institute of Technology's Tech Model Railroad Club, who were using a computer to control their train layout. It is defined in the 1963 "Abridged Dictionary of the TMRC Language" as "One who makes...an article or project without constructive end." As personal computer users, we should remember that virtually all we enjoy today we owe to hackers. But despite its honorable origins—all the founders of the personal computer industry were self-described hackers—the term is sometimes misused by those who don't know better to mean a computer vandal, someone who illegally invades another's computer system, usually via modem, for mischief or profit. We prefer to call these people crackers.

half duplex Describes a type of computer-to-computer hookup (usually via telephone lines) in which each character you type on your keyboard is directly displayed on your screen and also sent to the other computer. It's the opposite of *full duplex*, in which each character you type on your keyboard is sent to the other computer, which in turn echoes it back to your screen for display.

There are no big advantages either way, and both systems are used; however, if you have your computer set to the wrong mode when trying to communicate with another computer, you're going to get strange results. For example, if you type "HELLO" and see "HHEELLOO" on your screen, you're in half duplex and the other computer's in full duplex. If you see nothing when you type, you may be in full duplex and the other machine in half duplex.

halftone Similar to dithering, the use of patterns of black and white dots that fool the eye into seeing gray. The difference is that in a dithered picture the dots are all the same size, but they're spaced closer together or further apart to achieve lighter or darker tones. In a  halftone, on the other hand, they're clustered into a regular grid of larger and smaller black clumps. Since almost all current Macintosh printers can only print solid black—not gray—dots, dithering or halftoning is the only way to simulate gray on paper (other than using a badly worn ribbon or toner cartridge).

handle A small marker displayed on the screen that tells you a graphic object is *selected*. Handles are usually small black squares; you'll see them shown at the corners (and sometimes on the edges) of a selected object. By dragging on the handles, you can resize or reshape the object. Handles are shown on the screen only for your convenience; they will never print out on paper.

handshaking Two-way communication between a computer and an accessory such as a *modem* or printer. For example, instead of just blindly sending a continuous stream of text to a printer and running the risk of overwhelming it with data, your Macintosh sends data while watching a handshaking signal from the printer. If the printer has more than it can handle, it sends a signal that means "Stop! I've got all I can cope with right now!" When the signal comes on, the Mac stops sending until the printer has had a chance to print out the text it's working on. When the printer is ready for more, it turns off the handshaking signal, whereupon the Mac resumes sending.

hang See *freeze*.

hanging indent A way of formatting text so that the first line of each paragraph is offset to the left (sometimes called an *outdent*). This dictionary is set with hanging indents.

hard copy A physical printout on paper or film, as opposed to the electronic image you see on your screen.

hard disk A large-capacity data storage device that uses rapidly spinning rigid metal platters to store information. Each platter is coated with magnetic oxide; the basic read/write/erase method is similar to that used in a tape recorder. Because the information is stored magnetically, hard disks remember even when power is off, unlike *RAM* (memory). Hard disks are about ten thousand times slower than RAM, taking thousandths of a second to read or write where RAM takes billionths. They are, however, about ten to twenty times faster than *floppy disks*.

hard hyphen A hyphen that the program never hides. Take the name "Mrs. Alexis Smythe-Jones." You'd want that hyphen to stay there, even if the name was in the middle of a line. By contrast, a *soft hyphen* will remain invisible unless the word containing it gets pushed up to the end of a line. Then the word will break at the soft hyphen, which will be displayed.

hard return Occurs when you press the return key and the text entry point is forced down to the beginning of the next line. A hard return is often used in a page layout program or with a word processor to begin a new paragraph. If you format a document with either an *indent* or extra space between paragraphs, a hard return is inserted automatically.

hardware The electrical/mechanical part of a computer. We tend to focus on it, forgetting that it's useless without *software*. Good hardware is relatively easy to build; good software is tough to write. Just look at IBM: their  hardware is fine, but their software is so ugly that they ended up buying Apple's *Pink* code as the basis of their advanced operating system! (See *Taligent.*)

hardwired Not easily changeable, not programmable. Usually said of a program, as in, "It would be nice if you could customize the type size, but that feature is hardwired."

Hayes compatible Functionally equivalent to the industry standard D.C. Hayes *modems*. In particular, a modem that understands the Hayes command language and will dial, change settings, and so forth in response to standard commands like ATDT 555-1212. For practical purposes, a modem that's not Hayes-compatible is worthless. Fortunately there aren't many around, but if someone offers you a too-good-to-be-true deal, especially on an older modem, it pays to make certain!

header Text (or sometimes graphics) appearing at the top of each page of a multipage document. For example, many books have a header consisting of the book title at the top of each left-hand page and the chapter name at the top of each right-hand page.

HEPP (HEP) Higher Education Purchase Plan. A program whereby students, faculty, and staff of selected colleges and universities can purchase Apple equipment at about two-thirds of list price.

Hertzfeld, Andy One of the Mac's original software geniuses, Andy wrote many clever programming "hacks" that became part of the Mac *operating system*. For example, his brilliant Switcher program allowed you to load as many as four programs at once and jump from one to another in instants—it was the predecessor of MultiFinder. What was truly remarkable was that it let you do this with just 512K of *RAM!* Here's Andy describing himself back in 1984: "I'm an outlaw-type mentality. I like it when people say, 'No, it's impossible to do that.' That makes me want to do it." The *hacker's* credo in a nutshell—and that's Andy's philosophy. Truth is, all of the Mac's founding mothers and fathers thought more or less this way—that's what made the Mac the Mac.

hexadecimal A number expressed in base-16 notation, like 2A0F. Our familiar decimal system uses ten characters (0 through 9) and counts in powers of ten. The hexadecimal system uses 0 through 9 plus A through F, and counts in powers of sixteen. Programmers often use hex notation because it's less cumbersome than *binary*, but is easily converted to and from binary (the counting system used by the Mac itself). For reasons known only to Motorola, hex numbers are traditionally preceded by a dollar sign, as in $8FC00.

HFS Hierarchical Filing System. The method now used by the Macintosh *Finder* to organize and display your files. Many years ago the original Mac used a system known as *MFS*, which was much simpler and less useful with large disks (especially *hard disks*). The two systems are different, but all current Macs can still read MFS disks.

hierarchical Arranged in levels, often in order of importance. Each level contains all levels beneath it. In the *Finder*, each level of the hierarchy corresponds to a folder. For example, the hierarchy "My hard disk:Documents: Dictionary folder:Macintosh Dictionary" describes the location of this dictionary as I'm working on it.

high-level language Vague, arbitrary term for a computer language that's relatively close to a natural language like English. Assembly language, which deals intimately with the nitty-gritty bits and bytes of a *microprocessor*, is a low-level language. *HyperTalk*, which can sometimes sound almost like English, is a high-level language. Languages like *C* fall somewhere in between and are the subject of long, passionate arguments among the computer cognoscenti.

highlighting The Mac's way of indicating that an object (text, picture, or whatever) is selected: by changing black to white and vice versa. Color Macs can be customized to use other highlighting schemes—I've seen some that would make Peter Max blush—but most users stick to the tried and true black to white method.

hint A specialized usage related to *PostScript* and *TrueType* typefaces. It's tough to convert a font's curves into the bitmapped characters needed for screen display or printing at small sizes (see *rasterize* for the details). As a result, these typefaces have added hints—bits of program code, actually—that come into play only at small sizes and low (300 *dpi* and under) resolutions and help produce better-looking characters. On high-resolution printers and *imagesetters*, they're ignored. TrueType and *Type 1* PostScript fonts are hinted; *Type 3* PostScript fonts are not.

host A computer that's set up to let other computers (called *guests*) use its files. They do this by connecting to it via a *network* and using special software like *AppleShare*.

H-P Hewlett-Packard, a company best known in the Mac world for its excellent ScanJet *scanners* and DeskWriter *inkjet* printers.

HyperCard Means different things to different people. It's an electronic Rolodex; a toolkit for customizing programs or making your own; a way of organizing information (like a small-scale *database* manager program); and a programming language, *HyperTalk*, which can be used to do just about anything you want. If you run into HyperCard's limitations, Aldus's SuperCard is a compatible program that goes way beyond what HyperCard can do.

HyperTalk A computer language built into HyperCard. It's English-like, easy to learn and use, and powerful (but not especially fast). An example is the HyperTalk statement "If age is greater than 39 then subtract 10 from age"—pretty easy to understand even if you're not a programmer!

Hz (HERTZ) Hertz, a unit equal to one repetition per second. For example, a 60-Hz alternating current signal goes through 60 positive-to-negative cycles each second.

Ii

IAC InterApplication Communication. A way for programs (applications) to send messages to each other. For instance, your *spreadsheet* program might command your telecommunications program to dial up Dow Jones and get the latest stock prices, so that it can automatically plug the values into a financial statement. It does this by sending an *AppleEvent* message that tells the other program what to do.

I-beam A *cursor* shape indicating that you're ready to edit text. Moving the I-beam cursor to a place in a text document and clicking establishes a flashing *insertion point;* whatever you type will appear there.

IBM International Business Machines. Apple's ancestral enemy and current ally, IBM pioneered the commercial use of computers in the 1950s with machines like the vacuum tube-based Model 650. For decades it dominated the business world with giant *mainframe* computers like the System/360. When it introduced the IBM PC in 1981, history seemed about to repeat itself: the PC quickly became the basis of a huge boom in personal computers. Established microcomputer builders like Apple were caught by surprise as the PC wave surged over them, leaving machines like the *Apple II* drifting in the backwaters.

But IBM soon found itself competing with hordes of PC-compatible machines—*clones*—that were faster and very much cheaper than its own products. Soon the giant began to lose market share, and eventually the clones dominated the PC market, with IBM scrabbling for a small piece of the spoils. IBM attempted to change the market's direction with the PS/2 models, with their proprietary Micro Channel Bus hardware, but failed—buyers ignored the new, incompatible machines and went on buying faster and better PC clones.

Meanwhile, Apple had surged back into technological leadership with the Macintosh, whose revolutionary software inspired a thousand imitators. Trying to leapfrog Apple, IBM announced the gargantuan (25+ megabyte) *OS/2* operating system, touted as the ultimate microcomputer OS, but was largely met with indifference—the majority of PC users chose *DOS* and Microsoft *Windows* instead.

Baffled, humiliated, and facing steadily shrinking sales and profits, IBM finally turned to Apple, forging an alliance in which "Big Blue" agreed to share its hardware expertise (specifically, its fast *RISC* processors), in return for Apple's advanced *Pink* system software. It remains to be seen who will get the most benefit from this marriage of convenience, or how long the relationship will last.

icon A small picture (for example, the Trash) that either symbolizes some action, such as throwing away, or represents a program or a document.

IGES (EYE JES) Initial Graphics Exchange Standard. A *format* for graphics files from older *CAD* (Computer-Aided Design) systems, especially those built around *mainframes* and minicomputers. Although it's a "standard," it's not really very well standardized, so compatibility and translation problems are common. Mac CAD programs can usually import IGES files, but generally use the *DXF* format to save their own files.

Illustrator A powerful *object-oriented* graphics program that sets the standard for professional graphics software. *Adobe* Illustrator has a deceptively simple, yet extremely powerful set of tools that makes possible very sophisticated graphics. Because it uses *PostScript* as its native language (after all, Adobe invented PostScript!), Illustrator can manipulate both type and graphics with equal ease. The Encapsulated PostScript *(EPS)* files it creates can be scaled to any size and printed at high resolution with superb-looking results. Most of the illustrations in this book were done with Illustrator, saved as EPS files, and then placed in PageMaker.

image processing A general term for taking images such as scanned or digitized photos from the outside world, bringing them into the computer, and modifying or enhancing them. For instance, you might have an old family photo with cracks and stains. After scanning it, you can bring it into an image processing program like Photoshop and retouch the picture to eliminate the blemishes and sharpen up the contrast.

Going a step further, you might even want to electronically delete your ex-husband from the picture. It's easy enough to do: just erase him, then clone the background to fill in the empty place left behind. (If only hearts could be mended so easily!) Obviously, the routine use of image processing tools like this by journalists raises some interesting ethical questions.

imagesetter A very high-resolution printer used to prepare *camera-ready copy* from *PostScript* documents. In the sixties this was done with phototypesetters, which used optical technology to project letters onto a piece of film but were unable to deal with graphics. Today's imagesetters from Agfa Compugraphic, Linotype/Hell, and others use computer-controlled lasers to do the job for both type and graphics. The principles are the same as in a common 300-dpi LaserWriter, but imagesetters have four to ten times the resolution—up to 2,540 dots per inch!

ImageWriter An old, slow *impact dot matrix* (mechanical) *printer*, capable of printing "near letter quality" text and graphics at up to 144 dots per inch. It came in normal and wide-carriage versions.

ImageWriter II Similar in capabilities to the original ImageWriter I, but a tad faster, sleeker looking, and could use a four-color ribbon and cut sheet feeder accessory. It came in a normal carriage version only; no wide-carriage version was available.

ImageWriter LQ A large, unreliable, very noisy *impact dot matrix printer* that can print 216 dots per inch, yielding higher quality text than

LQ ImageWriter

the ImageWriter I or II. Wide carriage was standard. Known inside Apple as "the printer from hell," this is the only product in Apple history to be recalled for modifications—and then recalled again to fix the problems created by the first recall!

IMHO In My Humble Opinion. *Telecommunications* shorthand.

impact printer A printer that makes its characters by striking an inked ribbon with hammers or pins, as opposed to a nonimpact printer using laser or thermal technology. Impact printers fall into two classes: 1) the now-obsolete daisywheel printers, which used a spinning wheel with each character on a separate petal; and 2) the still-common *impact dot matrix printers* (such as Apple's *ImageWriters*), which use an array of nine or twenty-four tiny pins to form characters from dots.

implement In the computer world, this means to make, do, or build, as in, "We plan to implement that feature in our next release." (Translation: "We haven't figured out how to do that yet.")

implementation In the computer world, a way of doing things, as in, "This is the lousiest implementation of print *spooling* I've ever seen!"

incremental backup If you saved every file on your *hard disk* each time you backed up, it would be a painful, time-consuming process. Fortunately, that's not necessary. Smart *backup* programs like DiskFit and Retrospect can look at all the files on your disk, see which ones have been changed since the last backup, and save only those files. Backing up "incrementally" in this way cuts the process down to an easy couple of minutes, since a typical user's 80 MB hard disk has only a few hundred K worth of changed files at the end of a working day.

indent To add some white space at the left of a line of text, as is often done with the first line of a paragraph. In the bad old days, folks did this by slamming the spacebar on the trusty old Smith-Corona a few times, or maybe by hitting the tab key, but those methods are way out of date. Computers make life easier: just drag the indent marker on your word processor's ruler, and the white space will be added automatically. Nowadays, indenting with spaces or tabs will get you a well-deserved lecture from the poor editor who has to waste time stripping out the unneeded characters—so don't do it!

infinite loop See *endless loop*.

information service A large commercial computer system, like *AOL, CompuServe,* or *GEnie,* which acts as an information resource for its subscribers. If you can imagine a cross between a bookstore, a public library, and a bulletin board, you have a hint of what this is like. A typical information service includes a large computer *network* and has hundreds of thousands of subscribers. You can call in with your computer and a *modem* connected to your phone line; for an hourly fee (typically five to ten dollars), you can *download* free programs, read the news from various wire services, track your investments, shop, send mail, ask for help with computer problems, and much more.

INIT (IH NIT) Old term for an *extension,* a small piece of software that's loaded at startup and modifies the *operating system*.

initialize To erase a disk (either hard or floppy) completely and prepare it for new data. Don't do this unless you're really sure you want to wipe everything off the disk!

inkjet A kind of printer that uses tiny nozzles to squirt microscopic droplets of ink at the paper, creating letters and graphics. Sounds crazy, but it works—inkjet printers like Hewlett-Packard's DeskWriter are the most economical way to get 300-dpi printouts from your Mac. The

77

downside: they're slow—in the case of Apple's StyleWriter, almost unbelievably slow—and you'd better keep those pages dry, because the ink can run when moist!

insanely great Really terrific; so wonderful you'll go crazy over it. A catchphrase at Apple when the Mac was being developed—if a feature wasn't insanely great, then it wasn't good enough.

insertion point The flashing verti- Insert text h|re
cal line that indicates where text will
be inserted when you start typing. To move the insertion point, just move the *cursor* to the spot you want and click the mouse. Remember, text will be inserted at the insertion point, not at the cursor! (This often confuses former MS-DOS users.) Sometimes folks mistakenly refer to the insertion point as a cursor, but the cursor has a completely different function.

Inside Macintosh A series of books recently revised in a big way by Apple Computer that defines the Mac hardware and operating system software. Considered the bible of Mac programmers, the series is more often talked about than read, because in order to understand any one part, you need to have already read all the other parts—a logical impossibility.

Installer A program that makes it relatively painless to update your operating system to the latest version. Always use the Installer to do this—never just drag the new files into your *System Folder!* Here's a useful, undocu- Installer
mented feature: if you get into the Installer's Custom Install screen and hold down the Option key, it changes into a Remover! If you install a new system and then discover that your bread-and-butter applications are incompatible with it, this trick will let you remove it completely, after which you can reinstall the older version.

Other installers are also used to install large, complex programs like PageMaker, which require many files to be copied to your hard disk in various places. An Installer does this for you automatically, making the task easy.

Don't ever try to just drag a program like this onto your disk. In days gone by, you could get away with that approach, but nowadays things are too complex. Let the Installer do the job.

interactive Somewhat vague buzzword used to mean "user-controllable." For instance, a movie you see in a theater is not interactive—the story unfolds on the screen in a strictly predetermined sequence, and all you can do is passively watch (or walk out). By contrast, a Nintendo video game is interactive: what happens on the screen depends on what you do.

interface 1) The circuitry (usually, but not always, built in) needed to make different computer accessories "talk" to each other. Think of it as something that translates electrical signals from one type to another type. You don't need an interface to connect your mouse to your Mac, but some older H-P *scanners* needed a special external interface box to adapt their proprietary *bus* for use with the Mac's *SCSI* bus. You would also need a special interface box if you were planning to hook up a *parallel* printer to the Mac's *serial* printer connector.

2) The way a program interacts with its user, more properly called its *user interface*.

interlace A way of displaying low-resolution pictures on a TV screen while minimizing flicker. Each image, or *frame*, is made up of hundreds of horizontal scan lines. Instead of displaying them in 1-2-3, top-to-bottom order, an interlaced frame is displayed as two fields: first, all the even-numbered lines are shown, then all the odd-numbered ones are drawn in between them. Why go to all this trouble? Because the screen is redrawn twice as often, interlacing reduces annoying flicker. But because it's hard to get the two fields to interlace precisely with each other, vertical resolution tends to suffer. Normal broadcast TV is interlaced, using the old *NTSC* video standard; some non-Mac computer displays also use this system. All Mac displays are noninterlaced, for optimum picture quality.

interleave The way in which successive chunks of information are written on a *hard disk drive*, depending on the speed of your computer. With current Macs, blocks of data can be stored one *sector* after another (called "1:1 interleave"), because the Macs are fast enough to read and write them that way as the disk spins.

If a drive formatted this way is connected to an old, slow Mac Plus, however, the computer reads one sector, then takes so long to store the information in memory that it can't catch the following sector in time; instead, it has to wait for the drive to spin a full revolution and catch it on the next go-around. This slows things down considerably. To work best with the Plus, the drive needs to be formatted 1:3 so that the Mac will read a sector, digest the information while the next two sectors go by, then read another sector and so forth.

Ideally, then, a hard disk drive should be formatted at an interleave that matches the computer it's to be used with: 1:1 for all current Macs, 1:2 for older 68000-based SEs, and 1:3 for Mac Pluses. A mismatched drive and computer will work, but you'll pay a penalty in speed.

Internet A large, international *network* of thousands of computers running the *Unix operating system*. Most Internet users are affiliated with colleges and universities, a few with large corporations or government. Almost no private individuals are on the Internet; it just costs too much. The Internet's software is fairly primitive by today's standards—it's strictly text-based and supports only 7-bit data transfers—but the system is so large that it has become a standard of sorts.

interpolation Educated guesswork based on known values. For example, if the temperature at 2:00 p.m. was 56° and the temperature at 3:00 was 60°, you could figure by interpolation that the temperature at 2:30 must have been around 58°. Interpolation is used in graphics programs to recreate missing data. For example, by looking at the *pixels* in two adjacent scan lines, a program can interpolate the values and create a line in the middle, doubling the vertical resolution of the image. Of course, this is still guesswork—but the guesses are right more often than not.

interpreter A program (like *HyperCard* or *BASIC*) that takes a user-written computer program, translates it to low-level instructions that the *microprocessor* can execute, and carries them out—all "on the fly." (Think of a simultaneous translator working at the UN.) The alternative is to use a *compiler*, which does only the translation and presents you with a ready-to-run, double-clickable program. (Think of a translator creating an English version of a German poem, then handing you the manuscript to read.) Interpreters are very convenient to work with because you can interrupt the process at any point to make changes or to *debug*. However, since the translation takes substantial time, your program runs much more slowly under an interpreter. Although a compiler is less handy to use, the *standalone* applications it produces can run very fast because the translation has already been taken care of.

interrupt button The button next to the *reset* button, found either on the left side or the front of most Macs (depending on which model you own). When you press it, it interrupts whatever is going on and switches you into a mini-*debugger* window, where if you know what you're doing you can look directly at the contents of memory (displayed in *hexadecimal* format, of course!) and do other macho programmer kinds of things. For the average user, there's only one time you might need the interrupt button: when a program freezes and you can't quit, you can press interrupt and then type "SM 0 A9F4", hit return, then type "G 0" and hit return again. About one time in three this magical incantation will get you back to the Finder; the rest of the time you'll still be frozen and you'll have to hit the reset button. However, if you're running System 7 there's a more reliable remedy for program freezes: hold down Shift, Option and Command and press *escape*. That'll get you back to the Finder about three times out of four, so always try it before you try interrupting.

intuitive   An industry buzzword, now so broadly used as to be almost meaningless; originally meant "easy to figure out without reading the instructions."

I/O   Abbreviation for Input/Output.

ISDN   Integrated Services Digital Network. A medium-speed standard for sending both voice and computer data over the telephone system in *digital* form, bypassing the need for slow, inaccurate *modems*. ISDN gives you two data channels, each good for 64 kbps (kilobits per second), plus a lower-*bandwidth* control channel. That's faster than any modem, but not fast enough for real-time video. ISDN is available only if your telephone company has installed new, expensive equipment, so don't hold your breath waiting for it.

italic   A style of *serif* type based on the designs of Aldus Manutius, whose slanted characters   *italic*
were patterned after hand lettering done with a broad-tipped pen. The word italic is often misused to refer to any type that's slanted to the right *(such as this)*, but such *sans-serif* designs are more properly called *obliques* (as in "Helvetica oblique"). If it slants and looks hand lettered, it's italic; if it just slants, it's oblique.

Jj

jaggies Visible "stairsteps" in diagonal or curved lines, resulting from the fact that all computer images are built  up from square pixels. The higher the resolution of your screen or printer, the less obtrusive the jaggies will be—but they will never go away entirely.

Jobs, Steve Often described as charismatic, Jobs was always a better salesman than engineer, so it was no surprise when in 1975 he and his pal Steve *Wozniak* left their jobs at Hewlett-Packard to sell Apple I microcomputer kits to their fellow hackers. But after successfully evangelizing the *Apple][* to a position at the top of the sales charts, Jobs let it slip back to also-ran status after IBM introduced their enormously successful PC in 1981.

Looking for a way to leapfrog IBM, Jobs took control of an existing small-computer research group at Apple. Incorporating novel *interface* ideas borrowed from *Xerox's* Palo Alto Research Center (PARC), he spearheaded the development of the first Macintosh. The Mac group worked outside of normal Apple channels and flew a pirate flag above their offices—a typical Jobs touch designed to inspire the tightly-knit group.

Spurred on by Steve's near-fanatical enthusiasm, the Mac team worked like Trojans to build a completely revolutionary computer; to an amazing degree, they succeeded. After a slow start following its 1984 introduction, the Mac gradually took hold and became Apple's main revenue source.

Intent on redeeming himself after John *Sculley* squeezed him out of the company he founded, Jobs founded *NeXT* and vowed to build a better Mac than the Mac. But while the NeXT computers had many advanced features, poor marketing and the lack of basic essentials like a floppy disk drive crippled their sales. At last report NeXT was struggling to stay afloat by licensing its software to other companies. Needless to say, however, Steve Jobs remains as enthusiastic as ever!

JPEG (JAY PEG) Joint Photographic Experts Group. A way of compressing large color *bitmapped* graphics to more reasonable sizes, built into the Mac operating system's *QuickTime extension*. For example, *scanned* color images can get very large indeed: figure that a 300-dpi scan has 90,000 *pixels* per square inch, and at 24 bits per pixel that's well over 20 *megabytes* for an 8" x 10" image! Obviously you're not going to fit very many of these on a standard 40-meg hard disk. But JPEG compression can reduce that same image down to well under a megabyte in size, making it a lot more manageable.

How is this seeming magic accomplished? Well, rather than devote space to describing the color of each pixel in a picture, you can use an encoding scheme that simply says, "This pixel and its next umpteen neighbors are all white"—information that can be stored in very little space. JPEG compression uses this and many other clever tricks to reduce the size of a file. Based on what's known about the way your eye and brain perceive images, it significantly compresses the image where you won't notice it (in large, solid-colored areas) and less where you will (in detailed areas).

But JPEG compression is *lossy*—when you decompress an image, you don't get back exactly the same image that was originally compressed. Depending on how much compression was applied, the decompressed version will have lost a little detail, and repeated cycles of compression/decompression can leave you with a noticeably degraded image. Thus, this technique must be used with some care.

justified Text with even margins on both sides. This is accomplished by varying the amount of space between words and between letters. Studies have shown that its uneven word spacing makes justified text slightly harder to read than text that's set *ragged right,* but many people prefer it for its more formal look.

Kk

K Kilo. A prefix ordinarily meaning one thousand; in the computer business it means 1024 (which happens to be 2^{10}). Generally used as a unit of memory, it's understood to be followed by *bytes*. "The first Mac had only 128K [bytes] of RAM," for example. 1024K bytes equal a *megabyte*.

Kaleida A joint venture formed by Apple and IBM to produce *multimedia* systems and possibly consumer electronics products. It's too soon to tell what will come of this, other than the usual flurry of press releases.

Kare, Susan Probably the world's best-known unknown artist, Susan Kare's work is seen every day by tens of millions who have never heard her name. She's responsible for the "look and feel" of the Mac, *Microsoft's Windows* for *DOS,* and the *NeXT* computers—the three major personal computer systems now in use.

Her background is in the traditional "fine arts"—she holds a doctorate in art history—but when former high school classmate Andy *Hertzfeld* recruited her to the Mac development group, she took to *interface* design as if born to it. As Resident Artist on the Mac team, Susan designed the *icons,* the original typefaces like Chicago and *Geneva,* and most of the other graphic elements that gave the Mac its distinctive look. Carefully editing bit by bit, she fine-tuned the designs for optimum recognizability. "I pay attention to every dot," she says. "If you like needlepoint, you'll love bit-editing."

Following Steve *Jobs* to *NeXT,* she was Creative Director of the new company and gave the NeXT interface its distinctive character, using the two available grays to their best advantage to produce a much-imitated 3D look. Moving on after two years to establish her own interface design firm, Ms. Kare was soon hired by *Microsoft* to give their *Windows* program a badly needed facelift.

K

The quality and importance of Susan Kare's work can be judged by the fact that every program written for graphically oriented computer systems like the Mac, NeXT, and Windows in recent years has been heavily indebted to her original designs. Every time you drag a file to the Trash, you're looking at a Susan Kare original.

kbps kilobytes per second. Used to specify how fast data can be sent over a network. For example, a standard *AppleTalk* network operates at about 230 kbps.

Kermit A way of transferring files from one computer to another over the phone using a *modem*. Developed at Columbia University, the Kermit protocol is especially good in situations where the phone lines are very noisy. Most Mac *telecommunications* programs support the Kermit protocol.

kern To bring two characters closer together in order to make them look better. Letters that slant in opposite directions, like "A" and "V," look too far apart when placed next to each other; kerning overlaps their spaces slightly for a more pleasant look.

WAVE
unkerned

WAVE
kerned

kerning pair Have you read the explanation of *kern?* Okay. There are many pairs of letters (like "To") that need to be kerned in order to look really good. A Macintosh font can include a table of "kerning pairs" like this, with information about how closely they should be kerned. Most programs ignore this information, but where good typography is critical—for example, in *page layout programs* like PageMaker and Quark Xpress—the kerning table is used to fine-tune the character positions. A font may have no kerning pairs at all or as many as a thousand, depending on how finicky its creator is. It takes a little longer to display and print a typeface with a lot of kerning pairs, but the results are worth it!

kilo A commonly used prefix meaning thousands.

kilobaud Thousands (prefix "kilo") of *baud*. (A baud is a unit of data transmission equal to one *bit* of information per second.)

kilohertz Thousands (prefix "kilo") of cycles per second (hertz).

KISS (KIS) Keep It Simple, Stupid! A much-needed reminder to all of us that complicated solutions are usually not the best ones. These words should be tattooed across the forehead of every programmer who insisted on adding "just one more neat feature"—and ended up creating a hodge-podge program like FullWrite or UltraPaint. The same rule of thumb applies to graphic design—take a look at the cover of this book for a good example of what happens when a designer forgets the KISS principle.

kluge (KLOOJ) Something jury-rigged or messy; a Rube Goldberg solution to a hardware or software problem. Usually used disparagingly—"Jeez, what a kluge!"—or apologetically—"Yeah, it's a kluge, but it works." Sometimes spelled "kludge," but always pronounced with a long "u."

K

LAN (LAN) Local Area Network. A group of computers, printers, hard disks, and other accessories, connected together so that they can do things like send files back and forth to each other, share a printer, or use a large hard disk, called a *server*, as a central storage area for programs and files. There are many ways of doing this, the least expensive of which is *AppleTalk*.

landscape A horizontal-format document (like a landscape painting).

laptop A portable computer you can set on your lap, roughly the size of a notebook, like the Mac *PowerBook* series.

LaserDisc See *videodisc*.

Laser Prep (Unnecessary with System 7.) A file which used to be required for printing to a *LaserWriter* under systems earlier than 7.0. It lived in your *System Folder* and contained instructions telling your Mac how to send information to a LaserWriter. You also needed the *printer driver* file "LaserWriter" in your System Folder, and both had to be the same version.

laser wars When several Macs are connected to one *LaserWriter*, they must all use the same version of the LaserWriter *printer driver* (see next entry). If, for example, one user has LaserWriter version 5.2 while the others have LaserWriter 7.0, each time one of them prints, the LaserWriter will reset itself and spit out another startup page, which takes about a minute. This situation, in which there's a conflict between different versions of the printer driver, is jokingly referred to as "laser wars." Since it wastes time and paper, it's something to avoid.

L

LaserWriter A *printer driver* file that lives in your *System Folder* and contains instructions telling your Mac how to send information to a LaserWriter.

LaserWriter

LaserWriter Font Utility A handy program Apple gives you with your system software, this lets you do several useful things.

For example, if you're tired of watching your laser printer spit out a "startup page" every time you turn it on, you can permanently disable that feature. You can also *download PostScript* fonts to the printer, and thereby speed up printing.

LaserWriter printers Apple has made several LaserWriter models over the years; "LaserWriter" refers to any of them. All of them are based on electrophotographic technology, a fancy word for what goes on inside an ordinary office copier. In a nutshell, here's how it works: A computer-controlled laser emits a sharply focused beam, which is scanned horizontally across a light-sensitive drum. (Ever hear the whine, like a tiny jet engine, as a laser printer starts up? That's the small, rapidly spinning mirror that does the scanning.) As the beam is scanned, it creates on the drum a pattern of electrically charged areas where the light hit. Next the drum is coated with *toner*—finely powdered carbon. Because the toner has already been given a static charge of its own, it sticks to the drum only in those places where the light beam hit. Pressing the drum against a charged sheet of paper transfers the toner image to it, and finally a *fuser* unit applies heat and pressure to permanently bond the black image to the paper.

Except as noted, all the LaserWriters listed here are 300-dot-per-inch printers, include *PostScript*, have 8-page-per-minute (maximum) printing *engines*, and can be *networked* via *AppleTalk*. Here they are in chronological order:

LaserWriter Apple's original *PostScript* printer was a breakthrough in 1985, for both its "near typeset" print quality and its PostScript language. Together with software like PageMaker, it made desktop publishing possible. It had four built-in typeface families and could be shared by many Macs via an inexpensive *AppleTalk* network—another first. It could be upgraded to a *LaserWriter Plus*.

LaserWriter Plus An upgraded version of the LaserWriter, it had 11 typeface families: Avant Garde, Bookman, Courier, Helvetica, New Helvetica Narrow, New Century Schoolbook, Palatino, Symbol, Times, Zapf Chancery, and Zapf Dingbats. It's sometimes described as having 35 *fonts* because all the styles are counted.

LaserWriter IISC A non-PostScript 300-*dpi* laser printer. Since it doesn't use PostScript, its ability to handle type and graphics is rather limited. No built-in typefaces; your best bet with one of these was to use Adobe Type Manager (*ATM*) with Mac-based PostScript typefaces. Unlike most LaserWriters, it connected via the *SCSI* port and thus couldn't be shared by several Macs via *AppleTalk*. However, it was less expensive than its PostScript brothers and sisters. Can be upgraded to a LaserWriter IINT, IINTX, IIf or IIg.

LaserWriter IINT An improved second-generation PostScript laser printer but similar in performance and features to the LaserWriter Plus, which it replaced in Apple's product line. Can be upgraded to a LaserWriter IINTX, IIf, or IIg.

LaserWriter IINTX Faster version of the LaserWriter IINT, this has a speedy 68020 microprocessor at its heart. It also adds a *SCSI* port, to which you can connect a hard disk for storing PostScript fonts. Can be upgraded to a LaserWriter IIf or IIg.

LaserWriter IIf Similar overall to the LaserWriter IINTX but includes *PostScript* Level 2 for somewhat better performance. Also features built-in *PhotoGrade* software for greatly improved *halftone* printing (usable only if you upgrade the printer to at least 5 MB of RAM) and *FinePrint* software for slightly better text and line-art resolution. Can be upgraded to a LaserWriter IIg.

LaserWriter IIg Similar to the LaserWriter IIf, but with a marginally faster processor, more memory, and a built-in *Ethernet* port for connection to large, fast *networks*.

Personal LaserWriter NT A small, relatively inexpensive PostScript printer. Overall specs similar to the LaserWriter IINT (so the same comments apply). This version is in a smaller package and can print only four pages per minute.

Personal LaserWriter NTR A small, relatively inexpensive PostScript printer. Similar in appearance to the LaserWriter Personal NT, but uses a *RISC* processor for much faster printing, and incorporates PostScript Level 2.

Personal LaserWriter SC A small, relatively inexpensive non-PostScript printer. Overall specs are similar to the LaserWriter IISC (so the same comments apply). This version is in a smaller package and can print only four pages per minute.

launch To start up a program.

Lava Lite An essential accessory; every Mac user needs one. This table lamp, in which colored blobs of viscous fluid slither squishily across each other, is the very essence of *analog*-ness. Place it right next to your Mac monitor, and when you grow tired from too much time spent in the *digital* domain, rest your eyes and brain by watching the lava flow for a while. A vital *ergonomic* aid in fighting off the dreaded Digital Doldrums.

LC Low-cost Color [Mac]. See *Macintosh*.

LCD Liquid Crystal Display. A low-power display device used in portable computers (among other places). It uses a chemical solution with an unusual property: if you apply an electric field to it, its molecules line up in a regular grid, like the atoms in a crystal (hence the name), and can either block or pass light. There are two common kinds of LCDs: the slow but inexpensive *supertwist* type (used in the *PowerBook* 100 and 140) and the more expensive *active* *matrix* displays (used in the PowerBook 170), which have better contrast and can be seen from a wider viewing angle.

leader character A character, such as a period or under-line, used to visually connect an entry in a table with a number, thusly:

Chapter 5 67

You'll typically see these in a table of contents, where they help lead the eye across the page from the chapter names to the corresponding page numbers. Most page layout programs and word processors let you create these "leader lines" as a variation of the tab function.

leading (LED ɪɴɢ) The amount of vertical space between lines of type (originally done with strips of lead, whence the name). Conventionally,

> This type is set with tight lead-ing: 10/10.

type is set at leading equal to about 120 percent of its height. For example, 10-point type is usually set so that there are 12 points between the bottom of one line and the bottom of the next; this is written 10/12, pronounced "ten on twelve." If leading is too tight, text becomes hard to read. To some extent this is a matter of taste, and depends on the typeface and size used.

learning curve A measure of how hard it is to learn something—usually a software package. Generally, a pro-gram that's difficult to learn is said to have a "steep learning curve."

letter quality printer A printer (usually an *impact dot-matrix* type) that can't produce really good-looking type. (For example, the *ImageWriter LQ.*) In days gone by such printers, usually producing about 150–200 *dpi*, were thought to be good enough for letters. Nowadays the standard for business correspondence is 300 dpi—any-thing less gives an impression of sleaziness, reminiscent of those sweepstakes mailings with their jagged-looking type.

license agreement The fine print on the envelope your program disks came in—all that teensy type you never read because you were in such a hurry to try out the program. You know, the stuff that says you don't really own the software, it's just being licensed to you; it isn't guaranteed to work or be good for anything; you're buying a pig in a poke; you have no redress if the program garbles your customer files and you lose a million bucks' worth of business as a result…in short, what's known in the trade as a "tough-luck" warranty. (For an actual example taken from Apple's system software license, see *disclaimer*.) Interesting, isn't it, how the auto companies can sell cars by bragging about how good their warranties are? Bet you've never seen a software company brag about its warranty in an ad! Could they be missing something?

ligature A pair of letters, like fi or fl, that are tied together. Why? Because they look better that way than when typed fi or fl. Most *PostScript* fonts have at least these two ligatures; you can get them by typing Shift-Option-5 and Shift-Option-6. Some fonts, like Adobe's Expert collections, have many more. Some programs will put these in for you automatically.

line art Artwork that's made up entirely of black lines, like a pen-and-ink drawing or an engraving; the opposite of *grayscale* or *half-tone* art.

link 1) Shorthand for an electronic mail (*email*) message sent on the *AppleLink* network, as in, "I don't know the answer to that one, but I'll link Joe at Apple Developer Services and see whether he knows."

2) A logical connection between two separate documents—for example, chapters of a book created in PageMaker.

lino (LYE NO) 1) Shorthand for *Linotronic imagesetter*. 2) To send a document to a *Linotronic*.

Linotronic (LYE NO TRON IK) A high-*resolution* printer made by Allied Linotype. Although it has many times the resolution of an Apple *LaserWriter* (up to 2540 dots per inch vs. the LaserWriter's 300 dpi), the Linotronic can use the same *PostScript* graphical language, so it can print the same Macintosh programs and documents. This means you can set type on the Mac with its *WYSIWYG* display, print proofs on the LaserWriter, then go to Linotronic output for publication quality—something that's difficult or impossible to do with other personal computers. The Linos are not the only high-resolution PostScript output devices, but they were the first and are still the most popular.

Lisa The Mac's predecessor. Because of its slow speed, unreliable floppy drive, $10,000 price, and radical new *user interface*, the Lisa never gained wide acceptance. The introduction about a year later of the less expensive, more compact Macintosh sealed its fate. Apple made a last-ditch attempt to unload their excess Lisas by cutting the price, renaming the machine "Macintosh XL," and providing a halfway sort of compatibility with Macintosh programs, but this was a disastrous failure, and the remainders ended up being sold off to Sun Remarketing where, if you don't know any better, you can still buy a brand-new, sorta-kinda-maybe-Mac-compatible Lisa for under a thousand bucks.

Local Area Network See *LAN*.

LocalTalk A simple way of connecting several computers together to share infor- mation and accessories such as printers. A small box plugs into the printer connec- tor in the back of each Mac, and wires connect the boxes together, forming a network.

Because Apple's LocalTalk uses hard-to-find, hard-to-work-with cable and connectors, it has largely been super-seded by *PhoneNet*-style hardware, which is electrically identical but uses inexpensive modular telephone con- nectors and cable. Even Apple uses PhoneNet to wire up its offices! LocalTalk is thus largely a historical curiosity at this point. Apple still sells the hardware, but nobody with any sense uses it.

lock To protect a file or disk from being changed, written to, or erased. For disks, you   ☐ **Locked**

do this by sliding the *write-protect* tab to the open (see-through) position. For documents or other files, you select the file, *Get Info*, then click the box that says "Lock."

log on/off In order to connect your Mac to another computer (whether via the phone lines using a *modem,* or by way of a *network)*, you must first establish a physical connection. The other computer then asks you who you are and requests a password. When you've sent this information and the other computer recognizes you as a legitimate user, it will let you use its facilities; otherwise, it's likely to hang up on you. Entering your name and password is called "logging on"; it's the computer equivalent of introducing yourself when you call up on the phone and say: "Hi, this is Joe Waldron from Synergistic InterGlom. Have you got a minute?" Similarly, logging off is the computer equivalent of saying goodbye.

logic board A printed circuit board with mostly *digital* parts on it. For example, the Mac Plus and SE had two circuit boards: a "logic board," which held the *microprocessor, RAM, ROM,* and other *digital chips* and an "analog board," which held the power supply and video circuitry.

LOL Laughing Out Loud. *Telecommunications* shorthand. Extreme form: *ROTFLOL* (Rolling On The Floor Laughing Out Loud).

look and feel Another way to describe the *user interface* of a computer or program, or the way it appears and behaves.

lossy Describes data compression schemes like *JPEG,* in which compressing and then decompressing an image yields a version that has lost some detail in the process. By contrast, a lossless scheme like *StuffIt* compression never loses a bit of information. Lossy compression squeezes files down a lot more (about 25 times with JPEG) than lossless compression (about 2–5 times reduction).

lpi Lines Per Inch. A measure of how fine the *screen* is on a *halftone* reproduction, and thus of how smooth it looks.

Mm

MacBinary A way of transferring files via *modem*. When you send a file in MacBinary format, a little packet of information is tacked on that includes the file's icon, its *type* and *creator*. Without MacBinary, any transmitted file (including an application) would show up on the other end as a generic document, which wouldn't be very useful. *Telecommunications* programs for the Mac use MacBinary automatically unless you tell them not to.

MACE (MACE) Macintosh Audio Compression/Expansion. A software scheme for reducing the rather prodigious size of *digitized* sound files. It's built into current versions of the Mac's system software.

Macintosh computers The original Mac was a simple machine with no options. But as customers demanded more power and more features, Apple responded with a trickle of new models that soon turned into a deluge. (Some of these were largely marketing ploys, with little real difference between them.) Be that as it may, here—as of press time—is the complete Mac family in order of release:

Compact Macs All have a 9" black-and-white screen and at least one floppy drive built into a small, luggable case.

Mac 128 The original Mac; had a 9" black-and-white screen, a 68000 *microprocessor* running at about 8 *MHz*, 128K *bytes* of *RAM* (a lot in those far-off days!), 64K of *ROM*, and a 400K *floppy disk drive*. Upgradable to a Plus.

Mac 512 Nicknamed the "Fat Mac" (at a time when half a megabyte seemed like a huge amount of RAM); just like the Mac 128, but with four times the memory. Upgradable to a Plus.

M

Mac 512Ke   The "Fat Mac enhanced"; like the Fat Mac, but with 128K bytes of ROM and an 800K ("double-sided") floppy disk drive. Upgradable to a Plus.

Mac Plus   Like the Mac 512Ke, but with 1 megabyte of RAM and a *SCSI port* for use with external hard disks (an important step forward). RAM can be expanded to 4 MB.

Mac SE   Slightly faster version of the Mac Plus; very similar, but has 256K bytes of ROM and adds an "SE bus" expansion *slot* for use with plug-in accessory *cards*. The SE was the first Mac into which you could put an internal hard disk drive. RAM can be expanded to 4 MB. Upgradable to an SE/30.

Mac SE/30   Fast small Mac; has a 16-MHz 68030 microprocessor, 68882 numeric *coprocessor*, 1024K bytes (1 megabyte) of RAM, 256K of ROM, an *FDHD* ("SuperFloppy") floppy disk drive, a SCSI port for use with external hard disks, and an expansion slot (not compatible with the slot in regular SEs!) for use with plug-in accessory cards. RAM can be expanded internally to 32 MB.

Mac Classic   Pretty much similar to the SE, but lacks an internal expansion slot.

Mac Classic II   Similar to the SE/30, but not as fast or as expandable—or as expensive.

Modular Macs   All have a 68020 microprocessor or better, and most have *NuBus* expansion slots. Unlike the compact Macs, the display is not built into the case, so you can mix and match computers and video monitors—color, black and white, small, and large. *RAM* in all these models can be expanded internally to at least 32 MB.

Mac II   First of the large, fast Macs; has a 16-MHz 68020 microprocessor, 68881 numeric coprocessor, 256K or ROM, an 800K ("double-sided") floppy disk drive, a SCSI port for use with hard disks, and six NuBus expansion slots that can accept plug-in accessory cards (such as those needed for color displays). Upgradable to a IIx or IIfx.

Mac IIx Successor to the Mac II; similar six-slot box, but adds a slightly faster 68030 microprocessor, a 68882 numeric coprocessor, and an FDHD ("SuperFloppy") floppy disk drive. Upgradable to a IIfx.

Mac IIcx Compact version of the Mac IIx; similar, but has only three NuBus expansion slots instead of six, allowing a much smaller case. Upgradable to a Mac IIci or Quadra 700.

Mac IIci Similar to the three-slot Mac IIcx, but has a 50 percent faster (25-MHz) 68030 micro- processor and built-in 8-bit *color* video circuitry. However, when used in 8-bit mode, the video circuitry slows down the processor to the speed of a IIcx— so if you really want speed, you need to buy a separate NuBus video card! Dumb engineering? You said it! Upgradable to a Quadra 700.

Mac IIfx Much faster (40-MHz 68030) version of the Mac IIx in a similar six-slot box.

Mac IIsi Relatively inexpensive Mac with 25-MHz 68030 processor; has built-in video circuitry. Has one expansion slot; can use a single NuBus card if you install a NuBus adapter board in the slot.

Mac LC The initials stand for "Low-cost Color." This pizza-box-shaped Mac with built-in color video was intended mainly for schools, where Apple hoped it would serve as a replacement for the aging Apple][machines—hence the availability of an inexpensive Apple][e coprocessor card for the LC, making it possible to run all that pirated Apple][software that seems to be floating around every classroom in the country. Has a 16-MHz 68020 microprocessor, but without a numeric coprocessor (standard in most other 68020, 68030, and 68040 Macs). Has one expansion slot; can use a single NuBus card if you install a NuBus adapter board in the slot.

Mac LC II Similar to the original LC, but with a 68030 processor.

M

Mac Quadra 700 Even faster than the IIfx, this has a 25-MHz 68040 microprocessor, but is packaged in a three-slot case like the IIcx/IIci models. Has built-in video circuitry (up to 24-bit color) and *Ethernet*.

Mac Quadra 900 Fastest Mac in current production, with a 25-MHz 68040 microprocessor in a five-slot "tower" case (meant to be used standing on end). Has built-in video circuitry (up to 24-bit color) and *Ethernet*.

Portable Macs These come in various sizes ranging from a hefty suitcase to a slim notebook, but all are battery-powered and have flat *LCD* displays, so you can use them while traveling.

Mac Portable A 17-pound battery-opera-
ted backbreaker with *active-matrix LCD* screen,
16-MHz 68000 microprocessor (same *chip* as
in the Mac Plus and SE, but running twice as fast). Came in two models: the original didn't have backlighting for the screen; the second version did.

PowerBook 100 This lightweight (5 pounds), Sony-built notebook-sized Mac has basically the same features and speed (not terribly fast) as the original *Mac Portable* (see previous entry). One difference: unlike the old Portable, the PB 100 has a *supertwist LCD* display, which is inferior to the Portable's *active-matrix* screen.

PowerBook 140 7-pound Mac with 68030 microprocessor and supertwist *LCD* display.

Mac PowerBook 170 7-pound Mac with 68030 microprocessor, built-in modem, and excellent *active-matrix* LCD display.

Outbound (various models) Not technically Macs, since they're not made by Apple, but they work like Macs, thanks to having transplanted Mac ROMs. A throwback to the days before Apple had a true portable Mac, the Outbounds—basically Mac *clones*—were tolerated by Apple because they filled a pressing need. They still have some advantages over Apple's *laptop* Macs, but their future is uncertain.

Mac XL Sometimes jokingly called "ex-Lisa," this is not really a Mac at all, no matter what Apple says. See *Lisa*.

macro A way of automating the things a program does, instead of doing them by pulling down menus and clicking on buttons. For example, suppose you have a text file and want to change all the occurrences of a double hyphen (--) to em dashes (—) and all the double spaces to single spaces. Of course, you can accomplish both with your word processor's search and replace command, but if you have a whole bunch of text files, the best approach is to use a macro program (like *QuicKeys*) to record the commands in sequence, then play them back automatically for each file.

MacWeek Indispensable, entertaining trade journal of the Macintosh industry. Often called "MacLeak" because of its uncanny ability to find and print info on "secret" and unreleased products. Free if you can convince them you're a "Mac volume buyer"; expensive (but worth it) otherwise. Editorial quality and reviews are excellent; it's remarkable that they can do this well on a weekly basis—and we're talking about a publication that runs over a hundred pages every week! (For the record, it's entirely Mac-produced; they lay it out in Quark *XPress.)*

magenta Shocking pink; one of the four *process colors* used in color printing.

magneto-optical A type of high-capacity disk storage that uses a combination of magnetic and laser technology to store hundreds of megabytes on a small disk. A conventional floppy disk uses a small electromagnet (called the *read/write head*) to magnetize small areas of the disk's coated surface. These magnetized areas represent data bits. Since the magnetic field can't be focused very precisely, however, there's a limit to how many bits you can pack in with this scheme. Magneto-optical disks use a different magnetic coating on the disk—one that can't be magnetized unless it's heated above a certain temperature. The magnetic field is left on all the time, but a finely focused laser beam selectively heats tiny spots on the disk, which then become magnetized. Since a laser beam can be made much smaller than a magnetic field, you can fit a lot more information on a disk this way.

mainframe A large computer, like the kind you used to see in the movies: rows of refrigerator-sized cabinets with spinning reels of tape and flashing lights, housed in an antiseptic-looking air-conditioned room. Such computers are usually shared by many users at once; when you dial up *AOL*, for example, you're communicating with a large mainframe that may be simultaneously in use by hundreds of others.

marquee Another word for the selection rectangle found in the *Finder* and in most graphics programs; it's called a marquee because of the "chase-light" effect, similar to the lights around a theater marquee.

math coprocessor See *coprocessor*.

MAUG (MAWG) Micronetworked Apple *User Group*, an online get-together of Mac users around the world who use the CompuServe network to keep in touch. This was the Micronet Apple User Group back in the days when what is now *CompuServe* was still called Micronet.

MB Short for megabyte; a little over a million bytes of memory (1,048,576, to be precise). Common mistakes: writing "Mb" or "Mg" for megabyte. Please note that "Mb" means "megabits" and "Mg" means "milligrams." A 40-milligram *hard disk* wouldn't hold much data, so please be sure you say what you mean!

megabyte 1024K bytes (1,048,576 bytes, to be precise). Often abbreviated "MB."

megahertz See *MHz*.

memory Usually refers to *RAM*, not *disk* storage. RAM is integrated-circuit memory: very fast, but it forgets when you turn off the power. Just to complicate things, though, there's also *virtual memory*, which uses your *hard disk* as a stand-in for *RAM* (memory). Just remember: "virtual" means "imitation." Real ("physical") memory is always RAM.

memory management Broad term for hardware and software that divides up your computer's *RAM* (memory) in such a way that several programs can run at the same time in different memory areas without affecting each other (important if one program bombs!). In recent Macs (Mac II and later), this function requires either a PMMU memory management chip or a 68030 microprocessor. Early Macs can't do it at all.

MFS Macintosh Filing System. A method once used by the original Macintosh *Finder* to organize and display your files. Because MFS was pretty simple-minded and bogged down badly when used with large disks (especially *hard disks)*, many years ago Apple switched to a system known as *HFS* (Hierarchical Filing System), which was much faster and more useful. The two systems are different, but all current Macs can still read MFS disks.

MHz Megahertz, or millions of cycles per second, generally used as a measure of a *microprocessor's* speed. A faster speed means the chip is working faster; thus, a 25-MHz *Mac IIci* is faster than a 16-MHz Mac IIcx. However, these comparisons are valid only for similar microprocessors (in the example just mentioned, both chips are 68030s). You can't use speed ratings to compare different families of chips; for example, a 1-MHz 6502 (the chip used in the original *Apple][*) is actually faster than a 2-MHz 8080 because the 6502 has a more efficient instruction set.

M

microprocessor The brains of your Mac, it has tens of thousands of microscopic transistors on a fingernail-sized silicon wafer, arranged to do the essential work of a computer. The most popular microprocessor "families" are the 680x0 series (68000, 68020, 68030, and 68040) by Motorola, used in Macintoshes; and the 80x86 series (8088, 8086, 80186, 80286, 80386, and 80486) by Intel, used by IBM and compatibles. Computers with microprocessors from different families usually can't run the same programs, but they can exchange documents.

Microsoft Largest software publisher in the world, and Bill *Gates'* private kingdom. They own the standard IBM *operating system, MS-DOS,* dominate the Macintosh application software market with best-sellers like Word and Excel, and still believe that *BASIC* is the best of all possible languages. In the Mac world, Microsoft is famous for writing software that doesn't follow Apple's programming rules; consequently, the software stops working every time Apple updates the Mac *operating system.* When Apple brought out the 68040-based Mac Quadras, for example, every single Microsoft product except Flight Simulator crashed on the new machines, because Microsoft had ignored Apple's rules about software compatibility. But hey! Why should they follow somebody else's rules? They make up their own rules as they go along.

MIDI (MIH DEE) Musical Instrument Digital Interface. A hardware and software standard that defines a way for electronic musical instruments and computers to communicate with—and control—one another. With an inexpensive MIDI *interface* and the right software, your Mac can control several synthesizers at once—a virtual computerized multitrack recording studio!

mini Short for minicomputer. A medium-sized computer, larger than a breadbox but smaller than a refrigerator. Or looking at it another way, faster than a *workstation* (or a Mac), but slower than a *mainframe.* Minis are often used as *file servers* on large networks. A common example is the VAX, by Digital Equipment Corporation *(DEC).*

MIPS (MIPS) Millions of Instructions Per Second. A very rough *benchmark* of a computer's processing speed, this is the 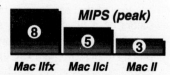 number of machine-language instructions it can execute in one second. Since it can take hundreds of these low-level instructions to do something as simple as multiplying two numbers together, MIPS ratings are not as impressive as they sound. But they can be useful in making a rough comparison of two computers: if one runs at 2 MIPS (like a Mac II) and the other at 16 MIPS (like a Quadra 700), you can be pretty sure the 16-MIPS machine is noticeably faster (though not necessarily 8 times faster). In short, like all benchmarks, MIPS ratings should be taken with a large grain of salt.

MNP Microcom Networking Protocol. Actually, there's a whole set of MNP *protocols* for sending information over phone lines rapidly and accurately, but the only two you need to worry about are MNP 4 and MNP 5. This is stuff that's usually built into your *telecommunications* software; computers on both ends of the connection need to understand MNP in order to use its features.

MNP 4 performs error correction. If data gets garbled in transmission, the MNP software detects the errors and makes sure the data is retransmitted if necessary. MNP 4 also improves transmission speed by about 5 percent. MNP 5 compresses data as it's sent in order to speed up transmission, then decompresses it on the other end. Since you're usually paying by the minute when you're connected to an information service, the less time it takes to transmit a file, the less it costs you. However, the efficiency of MNP 5 compression varies widely depending on the type of data being sent. With raw text you may get as much as a 300-percent speed boost, but with files that have already been compressed with a utility like StuffIt, MNP 5 can actually slow down transmission! MNP is strictly an American standard, and is generally considered inferior to the worldwide *V.32* and *V.42* standards.

MODE32 An *extension* that *patches* the Mac's *operating system* to correct some programming mistakes Apple made in the *ROMs* of older Macs such as the Mac II, IIx, and IIcx. The bugs in question prevented these machines from being able to use large amounts of *RAM*.

modem (MOE DEM) MOdulator/DEModulator. A device that converts the on/off *digital* signals from your Mac into high- and low-pitched audible tones. This makes it possible to use the telephone lines to communicate with other

M

modem-equipped computers—for example, commercial *information services* like *AOL* and private *BBSs*. Modems come in various speeds; 2400 *baud* was common until recently, but 9600 baud is becoming the standard. To use your modem, you'll need a *terminal emulator* program like Free Term or MicroPhone.

modem port The connector on the back of your Mac that you use to hook up a *modem*, a *Wacom graphics tablet*, or other *serial* input/ output *(I/O)* device). It's one of two serial I/O ports on every Mac; the other is the *printer port*.

modifier keys Keys like Shift, Command, Control, and Option that modify the meaning of the alphabetic keys. The Shift and Option keys let you type uppercase or special *characters*. For example, holding down Option while pressing the P key types the Π character—the Greek equivalent. The Command and Control keys, on the other hand, don't produce visible characters—but when combined with alphabetic keys, they're interpreted as commands. Command-Q, for instance, lets you quit most Mac programs.

modular Mac A Mac (for example, a IIsi) that has its video *monitor* and central processing unit *(cpu)* as separate modules, rather than combining both in one case like the Mac Classic.

moiré (MWA RAY) A shimmering effect that can occur when two similar patterns are overlaid. It's a common problem when output-  ting Mac images to videotape. Interference between the ever-present grid of video scan lines and things like the stripes in an active window's title bar can cause annoying moiré shimmer. To minimize the problem, try to avoid the use of single-pixel horizontal lines in any image that's destined for video output.

monitor Shorthand for "video monitor"; basically a very high-quality TV set with no tuner.

monochrome Black and white (no grays), as in 1-bit *color*.

monospaced font A typeface, like Courier or Monaco, in which all the characters ᴍᵢₗₘₑᵣ are exactly the same width. As you can guess, this one-size-fits-all approach leads to ugly, distorted character shapes—the "l" and "i" often have huge serifs to make them look wider, while the "W" is squeezed painfully to make it fit. Monospaced fonts are employed mostly by *DOS* users who don't know any better.

motherboard Slang for the main digital circuit board in your Mac. Smaller boards that plug into the motherboard (for example, NuBus cards or add-in upgrade boards) are called daughterboards.

mount In the old days, "mounting" meant taking a reel of computer tape and mounting it on the tape drive's spindle so the computer could use it. Nowadays it means making any *volume* (a floppy disk, *SyQuest* cartridge, tape cartridge, or even a disk *partition*) available to the computer. Usually this happens without your having to do anything—when you insert a floppy, it's always mounted automatically—but sometimes it's necessary to use a software utility to tell the operating system, "Hey! I want to use this volume now!"

mouse tracking The ratio of mouse movement to screen pointer movement. The Mac has a very sophisticated system: it moves the *pointer* about one inch for every inch the mouse is moved at slow speeds, but if you move the mouse faster, the pointer moves as much as two inches per inch of mouse travel. This allows you to have precise control when you need it for positioning things exactly where you want them—and when you need to get quickly from one side of the screen to the other, you don't have to move the mouse seven or eight inches across your desk. If this sounds like a trivial thing, try using a mouse-equipped *DOS* computer some time—there's a world of difference!

Mouse tracking can be set from the Mouse *control panel* to one of six speeds. If you have a large screen, you'll want to select one of the fastest settings. Think what it would be like having a 19" diagonal screen and needing to clear an equal desk area for mousing. It's hard to find a mouse pad that big! Fast mouse tracking saves you from that predicament.

MPEG (EM PEG) Moving Picture Experts Group. A standard for compressing digital video, animation, and audio files. Since these files, in their natural state, can easily run into many megabytes, some kind of compression is almost indispensable for serious work. For details on how compression works, see *JPEG*.

MS-DOS (EM ESS DOSS) Microsoft Disk Operating System. A primitive, non-graphical, user-unfriendly operating system used by IBM personal computers and their clones. Originally known as QD-DOS, for "Quick and Dirty DOS," it was developed by Seattle Computer Systems as a rudimentary disk operating system for Intel's then-new 8088 *microprocessor*. When *IBM* approached *Microsoft* with a request to create an operating system for the IBM PC (which was then under development), Microsoft bought the rights to QD-DOS rather than create their own DOS from scratch. A little patching up, and voila! we had the *kluge* known as MS-DOS. Masochists can run DOS applications on their Macs by installing a *coprocessor card*.

MTBF Mean Time Between Failures. In other words, how long before it breaks—on the average, of course! A statistical measure of reliability. Take it with a grain of salt, but all things being equal, a longer MTBF is better than a shorter one.

MUG (MUG) Macintosh User Group. See *user group*.

MultiFinder Old name for Apple's *multitasking Finder* replacement. Before System 7, this was an optional extra; now it's always there, letting you run several programs at once and switch between them in the blink of an eye.

108

multimedia Oh, lord. Do I really have to try to define this? Okay, okay! This tired old buzzword means almost anything that ties together computers and video, computers and audio, computers and animation.... For example, any Nintendo game has a computer, animated graphics, and sound; so by definition, it's multimedia. So don't be overawed the next time somebody tosses this one at you. Just remember, "Super Mario World" is multimedia.

Multiple Masters Often referred to as "MM," this is Adobe's clever way of making a more versatile *PostScript* typeface. A conventional (non-MM) typeface has characters with fixed shapes and usually comes in several versions: roman, bold, *oblique,* and so forth. By contrast, a MM typeface has one or more design axes: light to heavy, normal to oblique, *condensed* to *extended, serif* to *sans serif.* A set of *characters* can be generated with characteristics that lie anywhere along these axes.

Okay, so you can create zillions of different combinations of characteristics if you want to take the trouble. Let's face it, though—most folks probably won't want to bother making a Helvetica that's just ever so slightly less oblique than Adobe Helvetica Oblique. So what is this chameleon-like font technology really good for?

The answer is this: it's a key part of Adobe's fiendish master plan to achieve galactic domination by making PostScript a universal document standard. The technology to do this, code-named "Carousel," is meant to let you do something truly amazing: create a document and give it to someone who may not have the same fonts you do! Today, this is a recipe for disaster. Without the original fonts, the document appears with incorrect line breaks, page breaks, and so forth. But in the future, MM technology will allow these fonts to mimic the basic characteristics (such as width and weight) of the missing typefaces. Thus, the recipient of your document can view (and edit) a reasonable facsimile of what you had in mind. That's what Multiple Masters is really about.

M

multisync Describes a video *monitor* that adapts itself to several different kinds of video signals. Many video monitors can handle only a specific type of signal; for example, Apple's popular 13" color monitor requires a 640 x 480 *pixel*, 67.5 *Hz*, noninterlaced signal. Feed it anything else and you'll just get funny stripes on the screen. Multisync monitors, on the other hand, can work with various standards—different screen *resolutions, refresh rates*, and so forth. You pay more for this versatility, but it can be worthwhile if you want to use the same monitor with several different computers or *video boards*.

multitasking The ability to do several things at once (like a working mother); for example, recalculating a large *spreadsheet* "in the *background*" while you write a letter with your *word processor*. To do this, the computer shares its time among several tasks; while it's waiting for you to type the next word in your letter, it can be working on the spreadsheet. Background printing, or print *spooling*, is a simple kind of multitasking.

Of course, there's no free lunch: running three applications at once is going to slow down each one, because they're sharing a single microprocessor. Apple's *operating system* can do some kinds of multitasking, but if one application bombs, the others may come to a crashing halt. The only way to avoid this is to use *memory management (PMMU)* hardware to protect programs from each other and to write the operating system specifically to take advantage of it. Apple's *A/UX* does this and is a full-fledged multitasking system.

mung Mash Until No Good. To damage beyond repair, as in, "The program went bananas all of a sudden and munged my file." This acronym originated in the early sixties at the Massachusetts Institute of Technology, where the first group of computer hackers arose.

Nn

nanosecond See *ns*.

navigate To find your way around a program. Things like menus and onscreen buttons are meant to help you do this.

nested Stored one inside the other, like Ukrainian babushka dolls. The most common example is nested folders on the desktop. You might have a "Taxes" folder, nested inside it would be a "Taxes/1992" folder, and inside that could be still more folders for "Deductions," "Investments" and so on.

network A collection of computers (and sometimes printers) wired together so that they can exchange information. A common way to do this is with Apple's *AppleTalk*.

NeXT After being kicked out of his own company by newcomer John *Sculley,* Apple co-founder Steve *Jobs* decided the best revenge would be to build a better Mac than the Mac. So he started NeXT and brought out a line of technically advanced computers. But although the NeXT machines had advanced features like built-in CD-quality sound and Display *PostScript,* they were very late coming to market and lacked some essentials such as a floppy disk drive. NeXT hardware sales never really got off the ground; at last report, the firm was struggling to stay afloat by licensing its software to other companies.

node A computer, printer, or *server* attached to a *network*. Think of a node as a bus stop where data can get on and off the bus.

ns nanosecond. A billionth of a second. Your Mac can accomplish a surprising amount in this infinitesimal sliver of time! You'll hear this word thrown around when people are talking about *RAM*: "It's only a *Mac Classic,* so 120ns

SIMMs will work fine." Just remember, there's no sense in paying for faster RAM than you need. (Faster in this case means lower numbers, hence fewer nanoseconds.) Putting 60ns SIMMs in a Classic won't make it run any faster!

NTSC (National Television System Committee) The standard that defines broadcast and recorded television signals in the US, Canada, South America, and Japan. (Other television systems are the British *PAL* and French *SECAM* standards.) Created almost fifty years ago, NTSC is now showing its age rather badly. Low resolution and poor color accuracy are its chief liabilities; TV engineers will tell you that these letters really stand for "Never Twice the Same Color"! NTSC will eventually be replaced by high definition television (HDTV), but nobody knows just when.

In technical terms, an NTSC video signal contains thirty *frames* per second; each frame has 525 horizontal scanning lines. To reduce flicker, the thirty frames are actually sent as sixty *interlaced fields*: first, the 262.5 even-numbered scan lines are sent, then the odd-numbered ones.

NuBus (NEW BUS) An electrical and mechanical standard for plug-in accessory *cards*, especially those used by the *Mac II* family of computers (II, IIx and IIcx, IIci, IIfx, Quadra, and others).

NumLock A key on the Apple Extended Keyboard (see *USS Saratoga*) that forces the numeric keypad (those numbered keys on the right) to generate—guess what— numbers! Golly, what a swell idea.

nVIR (EN VEER) A common *virus* that infects the *System* and other applications. When an infected application is run on a "clean" Mac, it infects the System. After that, anytime an uninfected application is run, it becomes infected immediately. Because it occupies memory and disk space and can interfere with other programs, nVIR can cause crashes and other odd behavior. nVIR comes in several strains and variants; all can be detected and removed by antivirus programs like *Disinfectant*.

Oo

object-oriented 1) Images that are created from geometric objects such as lines and curves instead of from *bitmaps*. Object graphics are "resolution independent"; that is, a curve that looks jagged when seen at 72 dpi

bitmap

object

on the Macintosh's screen will be smooth when printed at 300 dpi on a *LaserWriter*. The same radius curve, drawn as a *bitmap*, would look just as jagged on paper as onscreen. Examples of object-oriented graphics applications are MacDraw Pro and Adobe *Illustrator*.

2) Incredibly overused industry buzzword for any programming technique that breaks up code into small, manageable pieces called (what else?) objects. Object-oriented programming is usually abbreviated "OOP." (That invites a wisecrack, but I'll restrain myself.)

oblique A style of *sans-serif* type in which the characters slant to the right, but lack the *oblique* hand-lettered, *serifed* look of true *italics*. If it slants and looks hand lettered, it's italic; if it just slants, it's oblique.

O

OCE Open Collaborative Environment. Apple-coined buzzword for an *operating system* that supports *groupware*, making it easier for several people to work on the same project. For example, reporters, staff artists, editors, and layout people all could work on sections of a newspaper issue simultaneously, using *networked* Macs.

OCR Optical Character Recognition. Most adult humans do this very well, but computers have a real struggle doing it at all: taking an image of printed text and figuring out what all those funny black squiggles actually stand for. To do this with a computer, you start with a *scanned* image of the text—a *bitmapped* graphic—and run a program that automatically analyzes it, extracting the text in a form your *word processor* can understand. This is very difficult to do, because it means that the computer must look at a not-too-sharp image and recognize all the letters and symbols it contains. Many letter combinations—like "rn" and "m"—are very difficult to distinguish from each other. If the OCR program is good, the result may be as much as 95 percent accurate, but there will almost always be a few errors. Still, it often beats retyping!

OEM   Original Equipment Manufacturer.

1) Those who build equipment and sell it to others, who may incorporate it into their own products—or just relabel it and sell it under their own names.

2) To sell equipment as an OEM. For example, *SyQuest* OEMs its removable hard disk drive mechanisms to dozens of companies, who put the guts into boxes with power supplys and resell them under their own labels.

offline   Not connected to another computer. For example, rather than type an *electronic mail* message while connected to (and paying for) a service like *AOL*, it's wise to compose your messages offline and then go *online* to send them.

onboard   Built in, as in "This video card has onboard *GWorld* RAM."

online   Connected to another computer, as in, "I don't have that info here, but give me five minutes and I'll go online and check on it." Usually the other computer is part of an *information service* or other large *network*.

AOL   CIM

OOP   1) Object-Oriented Programming. See *object-oriented*.

2) What you say when you realize that the Trash you just emptied contained your 1992 income tax files, which you dropped there by mistake.

open   1) To start an application, as in, "When you open HyperCard, the first thing you see will be your Home Card."

2) To prepare a document for use, as in, "Open the file 'Taxes 1992' by double-clicking it."

3) To open a *folder* so that you can see its contents.

open architecture A vague phrase implying that a computer system will be *compatible* with software and accessories from companies other than the original manufacturer. Historically, open architectures have promised far more than they've delivered.

operating system A program that tells a computer how to run other programs, copy files, use a hard disk, print documents, and so forth. The Mac's operating system consists of a number of files (principally *System* and *Finder*) found in your *System Folder*, plus programs permanently stored in the Mac's *ROM* memory *chips*.

OPI Open Prepress Interface. A standardized way of describing a document, OPI provides a link between Macintosh programs like PageMaker and expensive *prepress* systems from companies like Atex. In practical terms, you can create a document on the Mac, export it as an OPI file, then move it to a high-end prepress system for some sophisticated *tweaking*.

optical character recognition See *OCR*.

optical disk A disk that stores information optically or *magneto-optically*. Examples include *floptical* disks, *WORM*, *CD-ROMs*, *CD-I* disks and *videodiscs*. Optical disks can usually hold much more information than magnetic disks; for example, a standard 3.5" (magnetic) floppy holds 1.44 *megabytes*, but a 3.5" magneto-optical disk holds 128 megabytes!

optical scaling A way of adjusting a typeface's letter shapes when it's used at different sizes. Most current *PostScript* and *TrueType* fonts use exactly the same letter shapes at all sizes (although *hinting*, a crude form of optical scaling, can modify the small sizes slightly). In the

Hmfg
6 points

Hmfg
24 points

old days of metal type, however, a separate set of characters was cut for each size, and subtle modifications were made to the smaller sizes (9 points and below) to ensure readability. For example, small sizes had wider characters, larger *x-height,* heavier *serifs* and *stems* and more spacing between letters. *Adobe's Multiple Masters* technology makes optical scaling practical for PostScript fonts, so we'll be seeing a lot of this in the future.

option characters A whole circus of wonderful oddities built into almost every Mac typeface; you get them by holding down the Option key as you type. They include things like ≠ • ° ∞ § ∆ √. To find out what option characters are available, use the Key Caps desk accessory (be sure to select the font you're working with on the Key Caps menu) and hold down the Option key. Don't forget that Shift and Option together get you another whole set!

orphan A displeasingly short line of type, as when the first line of a paragraph ends up all by itself at the bottom of a page, or the last line appears at the top of the following page. Although there are heated arguments about the difference between an orphan and a *widow,* for practical purposes they can be considered synonymous and should be avoided.

OS Abbreviation for *Operating System.*

OSA Open Systems Architecture. Something vague and ill-defined that Apple and IBM are cooking up in the software kitchens of their collaborative venture *Taligent.* The idea is that in the future, everybody's programs will be able to run equally well on Macs, IBM computers, and other machines using this as their operating system. It'll be an "open system," see? Right. I'll believe it when I see it.

OS/2 Operating System/2. IBM claims this monstrous (over 25 megabytes!), sluggish beast is the *operating system* of the future. Well, they used to claim that—until they made a deal with Apple to codevelop Apple's *Pink* operating system. (See *OSA* entry.) Now IBM's customers aren't so sure where OS/2 (often jokingly referred to as "half an operating system") is headed. Then again, aside from those unfortunates who bought into it a couple of years ago, most of the computer world doesn't really care. Mac users are sticking with Macs, *DOS* users are sticking with DOS and *Windows*...so who wants OS/2?

OTOH On The Other Hand. *Telecommunications* shorthand.

Outbound A family of portable Mac *clones*. See *Macintosh Computers: Portable Macs.*

outdent Synonymous with *hanging indent,* a format in which the first line of a paragraph is offset to the left of the rest of the paragraph.

outline font A typeface stored as a set of mathematical descriptions (quadratic spline curves, if you want to get technical), instead of a collection of black-and-white bits (a *bitmap*). *PostScript* fonts and Apple's *TrueType* fonts are outline fonts. Outline fonts are great because you can scale them up or down to any size and print them on any device without getting those bitmap *jaggies*.

outliner Shorthand for outline processor, a specialized kind of *word processor* with features designed to make it easy to work with text in outline form (heading, subheading, and so forth—you know, that stuff you learned in high school). An outliner makes life easier for you in two main ways. First, it lets you temporarily *collapse* an outline so that only its major headings are visible, making it easy to see the forest without getting lost in the trees. Second, it lets you rearrange the sequence of your document by dragging or copying the headings—which always carry their subheads with them, whether or not the latter are currently visible.

overhead 1) A transparent plastic sheet placed on an overhead projector. You can print these in any laser printer, but be sure to use overhead sheets marked "For laser printers" or "For copier use," or you may experience a costly printer meltdown!

2) Excess computer time needed to perform behind-the-scenes "housekeeping tasks," which generally means slower performance for the programs you're working with. For example, working in 24-bit color imposes significant *processor* overhead, slowing you down considerably. When you're just doing *word processing,* it's best to stick with black and white.

overlay To combine computer-generated graphics with video from a camera, VCR, or other source. For details, see *genlock.*

Pp

packet A group of bits that's sent as a chunk over a *network* from one computer to another. A packet includes data plus source and destination addresses. Why not just send all the data in one long stream? Well, networks break data into packets so that several machines can use the same connection simultaneously. Imagine five people in a room. If everyone tried to speak at once, there would be chaos, so you have to take turns. And when it's your turn, rather than talk a blue streak without giving anyone else a chance to get a word in edgewise, you pause briefly after every sentence or two to let someone else speak. In other words, you break your thoughts into chunks—just as a networked computer breaks up data into packets, and for the same reasons.

page layout program A program that lets you put together all the pieces of a publication like a newsletter, a book, or a brochure. Text, illustrations, and graphic elements like *rules* or coupon boxes can be assembled on the screen and arranged into a pleasing overall design, then printed out as *camera-ready* pages, ready to go to the printer. The most widely used Mac page layout programs are PageMaker (more *intuitive*) and Quark *XPress* (more feature-laden). This book was laid out in PageMaker.

paint program A graphics program that uses *bitmapped* (as opposed to *object-oriented*) graphics to mimic the action of brushes, airbrushes, charcoal sticks, and other traditional artists' media. The original paint program on the Macintosh was Bill *Atkinson's* pioneering MacPaint; current examples include Painter and Photoshop.

PAL (PAL) Phase Alternation by Line. A standard for transmitting television signals used in Britain and much of Europe. (Other television systems are the US *NTSC* and

French *SECAM* standards.) PAL has better color fidelity than NTSC, but is otherwise similar in performance. PAL signals (from broadcasts, videotapes, or *videodiscs*) cannot be displayed by US TV sets.

palette Like an artist's palette, a palette in a Mac graphics program can hold the colors into which you dip your brush; stretching the metaphor a bit further, it can be a collection of tools. Palettes are usually *windoids*—small windows that float in front of everything else so that they never get buried under desktop clutter.

palmtop A computer so small that you can almost hold it in the palm of your hand (no larger than, say, 4" x 6"). Apple doesn't make any of these—yet.

Pantone Pantone Matching System (PMS). A standard way to specify colors. In the graphic arts business you need to be very specific—you can't just go to a printer and say "I want this trademark to be a kind of light robin's egg blue." Instead, you haul out your Pantone chart and find what you want, then you call up the printer and say "Make it Pantone 298." Printers and other graphics professionals all have Pantone-certified charts, inks, paints, and markers, and many Mac programs even claim to produce Pantone-calibrated colors on the screen. The key word here is "claim." There's a world of difference between glowing phosphors on a CRT and reflective inks on a sheet of paper, and a perfect match between the two is simply not possible. Still, the closer you can get, the less fiddling you'll have to do at press time.

parallel A method of connecting a printer to a computer, used by IBM PCs and *clones*, in which many bits of information are sent at one time. Because the Macintosh uses a *serial* (one bit at a time) connection, it won't work with most printers made for IBM-type computers.

parameter A variable; something that can be changed. For example, when baking a devil's food cake, your parameters are time and oven temperature; when using a *telecommunications* program to *log on* to a bulletin board system, your parameters are *baud* rate, number of start and stop bits, and *parity*. Many people misuse this word, saying "parameters" when they mean "limits." Please remember: parameters are NOT limits!

parameter RAM See *PRAM*.

parent folder A folder that contains another folder. For example, let's say you have a folder called "Mama Bear" and inside that is a folder called "Baby Bear." "Mama Bear" is "Baby Bear's" parent. But you probably didn't need me to tell you that, did you?

parity 1) A way of checking on data being sent over a *serial* connection (for example, by *modem*) to make sure no *bits* were garbled in transit. To do this, the sending computer takes each 8-bit *byte* and adds all its bits together. If the result is an even number, a ninth parity bit is set to 1; if odd, the parity bit is set to 0. The computer on the receiving end takes the incoming data, performs the same addition, and looks at the parity bit to see whether it is correctly set. If it isn't, there's a high probability that one or more bits were changed in transit, in which case it asks the sending computer to retransmit the data. This example describes even parity. Parity can also be odd, in which case the parity bit is set to 1 if the sum of the data bits is an odd number, or it can be ignored altogether (no parity).

2) A similar error-checking scheme applied to a computer's memory *chips*. Although often used in the *DOS* world, parity checking of this sort is almost unknown on the Mac. Modern memory is so reliable that parity checking really isn't needed. Since it raises memory costs about ten percent, Macs just don't bother with it.

park To move the heads of a *hard disk* drive to a safe location—away from the areas containing data. That way, if the drive gets thumped or bumped and the heads hit the disk surface, no important data will get *munged*. In older drives this had to be done manually, but all modern disk drives park their heads automatically on shutdown. Some even do it any time you haven't been using the drive for a minute or two.

partition 1) To use software to divide up a hard disk into sections (also called *volumes),* each of which  looks to the user like a separate, smaller hard disk. This can speed up operation if you have a very large (more than 100 megabytes) hard disk, since the Finder slows down when it has to manage a large number of files in one volume. Splitting a disk into several partitions or volumes means that the Finder doesn't have to worry about as many files at once, since it looks at only one volume at a time. By the way, Apple's HD SC Setup *utility* lets you create several partitions, but only one can be a regular Mac partition (the kind I've been talking about here). The others must be specially formatted for *A/UX* or other weird operating systems, which isn't really useful for most people.

2) The chunk of memory set aside for a program to run in when using *MultiFinder* or *System 7*. Even if you have 8 MB of RAM in your Mac, a program can normally use only as much as its partition allows. If you often get "out of memory" errors from a program, try increasing its partition size. You can do this by going to the Finder, selecting the program, and using the Finder's *Get Info* command to see its suggested and current memory sizes. Increase the current memory by a few hundred *K,* then try running the program again.

Pascal A computer language popular at the time the Macintosh was introduced. It's significantly more difficult than, say, *HyperTalk* to learn, but yields much faster programs. The Macintosh's *operating system* was originally written in Pascal, but Apple has since switched to using *C* for such work. Created by Swiss computer scientist Niklaus Wirth and named for the French mathematician Blaise Pascal, Pascal was originally intended only as a teaching language but was later expanded to a full-fledged development system.

paste An Edit menu command that takes the content of the *Clipboard* and copies it into a document at the current *insertion point* or replaces anything that's currently *selected*. The Clipboard remains unchanged, so you can paste from it again and again.

patch A minor modification to an existing piece of software, usually to fix a *bug*. For example, the *MODE32 extension* was a patch to correct some programming mistakes Apple made in the *ROMs* of older Macs.

path The route you take to get to a file on your disk; analogous to its mailing address. For example, let's say that you open the disk "My Hard Disk," and in it you open the folder "Silly Stuff," and inside that folder is the document "Jabberwocky." The path to the document is then "My Hard Disk:Silly Stuff:Jabberwocky." (Notice that we use colons to separate the elements in the path name.) That's a complete description that will allow any program to find the file, just as the address on a letter allows a carrier to deliver it to your house. Mac users normally don't have to remember paths or even see them, but the system uses them to keep track of where things are.

path menu In the *directory dialog* that lets you choose a file to open, you can click on the folder name to get a path menu. This useful menu shows

🗁 **Newsletter stuff**
🗁 **PMUG**
🗀 **Documents**
▦ **Desktop**

you what folder contains the folder you're looking at now, what folder contains that folder, and so on down to the lowest level of your disk (the *root directory*). The path menu lets you "climb back down the tree"—all the way to the root directory, if you choose. Why didn't they call it the "tree menu"? Search me!

By the way, a useful trick in *System 7's Finder* is to hold down the *Command key* while you click on a window's title. Doing so will get you a path menu that lets you go to the folders that contain this window's folder.

PC Personal Computer. Generally taken to mean a *DOS*-compatible personal computer (as opposed to a Mac). By the way, the original 1981 IBM PC was designed and built in Boca Raton, Florida, which is Spanish for "Rat's Mouth." Would *you* buy a computer from Rat's Mouth, Florida?

PCX   A low-resolution *bitmapped* graphics format popular in the *DOS* world; also called "PC Paintbrush" format, after the first program to use it.

peripheral   A major computer accessory, usually an input or output device, so named because it sits around your computer (at its periphery, so to speak). Keyboards, printers, plotters, *modems,* and *disk drives* are all peripherals.

Personal File Sharing   A relatively simple way to share files and folders with other Mac users on a *network,* this is built into System 7 by Apple. Using this feature, you can make someone else's hard drive appear on your *desktop* as an AppleShare volume and use it the same way you use your own hard drive. Once it's there, you can open it, drag files to and from it, and so on, in the normal way.

PhoneNet   An alternative to Apple's *LocalTalk* hardware for building *networks.* Unlike LocalTalk, which uses a hard-to-obtain, hard-to-assemble three-pin connector, Farallon's PhoneNet uses standard crimp-on phone connectors (those tiny blocks of clear plastic at the end of your telephone cords), which you can get at any supermarket or hardware store. Can you guess which system Apple uses in its corporate headquarters? Yup—they use PhoneNet!

Phong shading   A way of *rendering,* which is depicting realistic shadows and reflections on a simulated 3D object. (Named after the author of this rendering *algorithm.)* Other rendering methods include *Gouraud shading* and *radiosity.*

PhotoGrade   A clever system built into the *LaserWriters* IIf and IIg for improving *halftone* printouts. In a nutshell, PhotoGrade makes it possible to print halftone images (like scanned photos) at twice the effective *resolution* of a normal LaserWriter—106 lines per inch *(lpi)* instead of the usual 53 lpi. It works by rapidly modulating the laser beam in the printer to make finer-than-usual dots so that even a 300-dot-per-inch printer can produce halftones that look as though they came from a 600-dpi machine.

pica (PIE cuh) A unit of measurement used by printers and typographers; equal to ⅙ inch, or 12 *points*.

PICS (PIX) An old standard for compressing Mac-created animation files; superseded by *QuickTime*.

PICT (PIKT) The name for one way your Mac can store graphics, either on the *Clipboard* or in a document. PICT-format graphics can contain either or both *bitmapped* and *object-oriented* graphics. PICT bitmaps can be black and white, *grayscale,* or *color* (up to 32 bits per pixel). PICT objects are defined as commands in the *QuickDraw* graphical language—simple geometric shapes like lines, rectangles, and arcs. Unfortunately, PICT object graphics are limited in precision and cannot contain complex curves or special text effects; for high-quality work, a better choice is *PostScript* graphics.

Pink The basis of the *operating system* of the future? Maybe. Here's what happened: when Apple was putting together a list of features to include in *System 7,* they wrote all the "must-have" features on blue index cards (is this quaint or what?) and the "would-be-nice-if-we-have-time" features on pink cards. While the "blue" features—well, most of them—were being written into System 7, another team of programmers worked on the "pink" features, with an eye toward future system software. As it turned out, Apple and its legendary foe IBM, after considerable wheeling and dealing, agreed to cooperate on a joint future operating system—and the "Pink" code became its nucleus. Even as you read this, hundreds of Apple's and IBM's best systems programmers are laboring ceaselessly to bring this grand plan to fruition—sometime in 1995, by current guesses. Will they succeed? Stay tuned for the next exciting episode, kids—and in the meantime, remember to drink plenty of Ovaltine!

pirate A person who illegally copies software instead of buying it. This is stealing and it's called piracy. There's nothing romantic or daring about it, though. Although most pirates never get caught, their larceny costs the software writers billions of dollars a year in lost sales. The result, of course, is higher prices for everyone else. If you pay for software, pirates are getting a free ride on your dollar. Pirating software is illegal, dishonest, and happens to be grounds for firing at a number of companies. So just don't do it, okay?

pixel PI[X]cture ELement. A single dot on a computer screen or printer.

platform A type of hardware. When people talk about "cross-platform compatibility," they mean "the ability to run on different kinds of computers" (like Macs and PCs).

plug-and-play Describes hardware that's allegedly simple to set up. You just plug it in and it works (like a Mickey Mouse phonograph)—or so the ads would have you believe. In real life things are seldom that simple.

plug-in A small, modular software tool that adds functions to a program like Photoshop, just as various attachments add functions to your vacuum cleaner. Usually a plug-in lives in the same folder as the program itself. When the program is run, it loads the plug-in automatically. The tool then appears on a menu or a *palette*, just as if it had been part of the main program. Plug-ins are a convenient way of extending a program's features without rewriting it completely. Also called extensions, add-ins, or additions.

PMMU Paged Memory Management Unit. Circuitry required to keep programs from interfering with each other in a *multitasking operating system* like *System 7* or *A/UX*. Can be added as a separate 68551 *chip* to a *Mac II*. On the 68030- and 68040-based Macs (like the IIci), PMMU circuitry is built right into the *microprocessor*, so no extra chip is needed.

PMS Pantone Matching System. See *Pantone*.

point When talking about text, a point is a measure of type size (height) equal to $1/72$ of an inch, or $1/12$ of a pica—which happens, not by accident, to be the size of one screen *pixel* on the Mac. (You're reading 9-point type right now.)

pointer The shape that moves around the screen when you move the mouse. Different pointer shapes tell you different things about what's going on; for example, the wristwatch pointer means "Be patient—I'm working on it" and the *I-beam* pointer means you can start editing text. Synonymous with *cursor*.

popup menu A menu on the menubar is called a pulldown menu, because you pull it down to use it. A menu anywhere else—like in a *dialog box*—is called a popup menu

✓Tabloid
A3 Tabloid
Envelope - Center Fed
Envelope - Edge Fed
LaserWriter II B5

because it pops up when you click on its title.

port 1) A connector on your Mac into which you can plug a cable connecting it to an accessory like a printer or *modem*. Examples: your printer port, the *SCSI* port to which you can connect a hard disk, and the *ADB* ports for keyboard and mouse.

2) Contraction of "transport"; to convert a program written for one type of computer so that it runs on another; also, a program that has been so converted. Usually used disparagingly, as in, "That's a really ugly program—but then it's a straight port from the IBM version." Many software publishers from the *DOS* world have been guilty of porting programs originally written in typical IBM style over to the Macintosh, in the hope of quickly cashing in on the Mac market—but without bothering to follow Mac interface standards. The results have ranged from crude-looking to hideous, usually forcing a hasty rewrite after early purchasers complain bitterly about how un-Maclike the program is.

P

portrait A vertical-format document (like a portrait painting).

PostScript A powerful *object-oriented* graphical language that tells printers (like the *LaserWriter*) how to build the shapes of letters and pictures and print them on a page. Each character in a PostScript typeface like Bookman is actually a small PostScript program. Because the PostScript language has hundreds of powerful commands, programs like Adobe Illustrator can make the printer do tricks like rotated, curved, and shadowed text. PostScript graphics (including characters) are composed of lines and filled shapes made with *Bézier curves*, which are mathematically described by the PostScript language's commands. Although it's not often done, PostScript files can also include *bitmapped* graphics like scans. PostScript is as close to a universal graphics standard as we are likely to get anytime soon; it works with Macs, *DOS* computers, *NeXT* machines, and even *minis* and *mainframes*.

PowerBook See *Macintosh Computers: Portable Macs.*

power user Slang term for a person who knows a lot about his or her computer.

PRAM (PEE RAM) Parameter RAM. A small area of *RAM* (memory) that's kept alive by batteries even when the Mac is turned off or unplugged. This area holds things like the date and time, speaker volume, and which drive is the startup disk. If your batteries die (common with older Macs like the Plus), the contents of PRAM are lost and you may have trouble printing or getting a hard disk to be recognized. In that case, you need to *zap* your PRAM, which restores it to *default* values. To do this if you're running System 7, restart your Mac while holding down the Command, Option, "P," and "R" keys. You'll hear a second startup beep, then your Mac will start up as usual. If you're using an earlier system (like 6.0.7), hold down the Command and Option keys while pulling down the Apple menu and choosing "Control Panel." You'll get a message warning you that you are about to zap your PRAM. Go ahead and click "OK"—you can't do any harm, and it may cure your problem.

Precision Bitmap Alignment A check box choice in the *LaserWriter's* Page Setup dialog (to see it, push the Options button), this makes sure *bitmapped* graphics look their best when output on a 300-dot-per-inch printer. This is necessary because almost all bitmapped graphics on the Mac are created at the screen's normal 72-dpi resolution, and 72 doesn't go into 300 evenly. It goes into 300 $4\frac{1}{6}$ times, and that's a big problem because the LaserWriter has no way of printing four and one-sixth dots! The practical result is that while most pixels get turned into 4 x 4 dot groups, every sixth pixel becomes a 5 x 5 group. This causes annoying distortion, especially in patterns— try printing a gray bitmap and you'll see what I mean. The cure is to scale the whole graphic down a bit so that it becomes a 75-dpi image and prints nicely. And that's all that Precision Bitmap Alignment does: it simply reduces the whole page to 96 percent of its original size in order to make those bitmaps look good.

preferences A file that's used by a program to store its *default* settings, such as which fonts and ruler settings to use for a new document. Most programs let you change these defaults (usually by making changes to the settings while no document is open). The program then remembers your preferences in the preferences file (often called a "prefs file" for short). With System 7, prefs files are kept in the Preferences Folder, inside your System Folder. Sometimes a preferences file can be damaged and cause all kinds of strange problems. If a program starts misbehaving, one easy cure to try is to quit, throw away its prefs file, then run it again, thereby forcing it to create a brand-new prefs file. You'd be surprised at how often this works!

P

Preferences In System 7, this folder (inside the *System Folder*) holds the *preferences* files of your various programs.

prefs See *preferences*.

prepress A broad term for everything that happens between the time all the elements (text and graphics) of a publication are ready and the time copies begin rolling off a printing press. In between are such prepress tasks as typesetting, color separation *(color seps)*, layout, output to film, stripping, imposition, and platemaking. Computers are slowly taking over many of these functions, which were traditionally performed by skilled specialists. It's now possible to take a publication from initial design to offset plates entirely on the Mac. Mind you, that's not saying it's always best to do so! In some cases, the old ways are still the most efficient; it's important to judge each job on its merits. Falling in love with the "all-computer" approach can be costly in time and money.

presentation graphics The stupefyingly dull slideshows that businesspeople use to convince other businesspeople to invest money in their projects. In the past this was done with flip charts or overhead transparencies; now programs like Persuasion and PowerPoint let you use the Mac as a substitute slide projector. Unfortunately, while the methods of presentation get glitzier every year (with ambitious users now moving into full-scale animated razzle-dazzle), the content hasn't gotten any more interesting. Sort of like TV—the picture has improved, but the jokes haven't.

printer driver A file that lives in the *Extensions Folder* inside your *System Folder* and contains instructions telling your Mac how to send information to a particular printer. If you want to print to a LaserWriter, you must have the appropriate LaserWriter driver file in your System Folder; if you want to print to an ImageWriter, you must have an ImageWriter driver. Each printer normally has its own driver file, which shows up as a choice on the left side of the *Chooser*. If you're wondering which printer drivers you have installed, a quick look there will tell you.

printer font A *downloadable PostScript* font; that is, one that isn't built into your printer, but lives in your System Folder, waiting to be sent to the printer when needed. These days, printer fonts serve another function as well: they're used by Adobe Type Manager *(ATM)* for screen display.

BookmDem

printer port A connector on the back of your Mac to which you can hook up a printer; it's also used to connect to an *AppleTalk network*. It's one of the two *serial* input/output *(I/O)* ports on every Mac. The other is the *modem port*.

PrintMonitor A program that lets *MultiFinder* and *System 7* users print "in the *background*"—that is, get on with their work while the Mac does printing chores in its spare time. Technically, it's a print *spooler*.

PrintMonitor Documents A special folder (inside your System Folder) that's used by *PrintMonitor*. It uses this folder to store the temporary files it creates while you're printing.

process color If you want to print a photograph of a rainbow, ideally you'd like to use a different ink for each color. Depending on how subtle you wanted to be, that could mean hundreds of ink colors—obviously not practical! So how can you get all the shades and tints of the natural world, without using an infinitude of inks? By using a special printing process called *halftoning*. To simulate lavender, for example, you print small dots of magenta (bright pink) alternating with small dots of cyan (blue-green). In this way, all the colors of the rainbow can be simulated by overlapping patterns of dots in just four colors of ink: *cyan, magenta,* yellow, and black (abbreviated CMYK).

processor Short for *microprocessor,* the brains of your computer.

Prodigy When IBM and Sears set out to create an *information service*, this is what you get: it's basically an *online* shopping mall pretending to be an information service, with Big Brother monitoring and censoring everything—including, by their own admission, your private mail. Criticizing the system in any way is strictly forbidden here (accounts have been terminated for this—no kidding!). On Prodigy, the unwritten rule is "Shut up and keep shopping." The system is painfully slow, the graphics look like something from the seventies, and there's a parade of

P

commercial advertisements on your screen at all times. The joke is that hordes of *DOS* users think this is a really advanced, user-friendly system!

Here's a funny Prodigy story that shows how computer-savvy they are: at a recent Mac trade show, Prodigy set up a booth and gave away copies of their software on disk, along with free Prodigy refrigerator magnets. Hundreds of people took the free floppy and the magnet and threw both into their bags. Of course, when they arrived home, they discovered that the magnet had erased any floppies near it, including Prodigy's! What a great way to build customer goodwill!

productivity How much you get done in a day. Computers were supposed to enhance productivity—that's why we paid thousands of dollars for these things, right? And that's why we have to have to spend so much time reading books like this, installing software updates, troubleshooting SCSI chains…gee, I don't feel very productive right now, do you? About the best I can say is that the work I do at least *looks* better nowadays.

program Instructions that tell a computer what to do in order to accomplish a desired task. It's like a recipe, which tells a cook what to do—step by step—in order to make a cake.

programmer's switch On older Macs (like the Plus and Mac II) there's a little funny-shaped piece of plastic with two tabs that mounts on the side of the case. Even if you have one of these older machines, you may not even have a programmer's switch, because Apple's instructions warned you not to use it unless you were a serious programmer. Well, they lied. Install it (if you've lost it, ask your dealer for another one) and the next time a program bombs, press the *reset switch* (the one with the triangle on it). This is better than turning off the power, which is hard on your Mac's power supply if you do it too often.

proportional font The kind you're reading right now; it lets each character take up as much width as is comfortable for it. For

Wilmer

example, a capital "W" needs to be much wider than a small "l"; a lowercase "m" falls somewhere between the two extremes. The other kind of font—frequently seen on typewritten office memos, but never in books or magazines—is *monospaced*, where every character takes up exactly the same amount of room. Monospaced fonts, to put it bluntly, are ugly and tiring to read.

There is one place where proportional spacing doesn't work well, though: in numbers, where columns don't line up if different digits (like "1" and "3") are different widths. For this reason, even proportionally spaced fonts usually have monospaced numerals.

proprietary A hardware or software system that's available only from one manufacturer and works only with accessories from that manufacturer. The intent is to make you a captive customer, forced to buy everything from one source. For example, the NewTek *Video Toaster* uses proprietary fonts, available only from NewTek—and they offer only a handful of typefaces, compared to the 7,000-plus *PostScript* fonts usable by normal Mac programs. Are you getting the idea that proprietary systems are highly undesirable from a consumer's point of view? Good.

protocol A formalized way of doing things; usually this means a way of communicating information from one computer to another according to specific rules. For example, *XMODEM* and *MacBinary* are two commonly used protocols for sending files over the phone lines to another computer.

pseudo-static RAM To understand this, you first have to know what static RAM (SRAM) is. Static RAM is memory that retains its data as long as power is applied— as long as it has a trickle of juice, it just sits there and remembers for you. Since that takes very little power, SRAM is often used in portable computers. Dynamic RAM (DRAM), on the other hand, forgets unless it's periodically exercised (like every microsecond or so), which takes some power to do. It's cheap, though, so DRAM is the kind used in most computers.

Okay, now we're ready (finally!) to define pseudo-static RAM. PSRAM is really dynamic RAM at heart, but it has built-in self-exercising circuits that let it pretend to be static RAM. It's cheaper than true SRAM, but not as stingy with power—a reasonable compromise for many purposes.

public domain A creative work (like a computer program) to which the author has relinquished all rights, leaving the work free for anyone to copy and use. Many programs in *user group* software libraries are in the public domain; some others carry a stipulation such as "Free for noncommercial distribution and use only," in which case the author retains rights but grants permission for copying and use as long as you're not making money with or reselling his or her work. Still others are *shareware*, in which case the author retains rights, grants permission for the program to be freely copied, but requests that a voluntary payment be made if you use the software.

publish To make data available for other programs to use; part of System 7's "Publish and Subscribe" feature. Let's say you use a spreadsheet to create a spiffy 3D graph showing the upward trend in sales at your chain of fast-food restaurants, "Wingz 'n' Waffles." You publish the graph from the Excel document, creating an *edition* file. Then you use PageMaker to create an impressive annual report for the chain and you *subscribe* to the graph's edition, placing it in your PageMaker document. Now when your accountant gets the latest sales figures and updates the spreadsheet, the graph's edition is also updated and the annual report incorporates the change— without your having to re-import it.

Qq

QT   Shorthand for *QuickTime*.

Quadra   See *Macintosh Quadra*.

Quark   Common shorthand for Quark *XPress*, a large, very powerful, chronically buggy *page layout program*. Often called "Quirk XPress" by its users, but it's getting to be an industry standard for serious publishing work. *MacWeek*, for example, is entirely laid out in XPress.

queue   If you're using *background* printing, you can print several documents and then go back to work while the Mac sends them to the printer. The list of documents waiting to be printed is called the queue. You can use *PrintMonitor* to see the queue and rearrange the files' priority or even cancel printing on a file-by-file basis.

quick and dirty   Getting the job done in the fastest way possible, without regard for elegance. Examples: fixing a leaky fuel tank with chewing gum; using *TeachText* to do a user group newsletter.

QuickDraw   A special-purpose computer language built into the Mac, it's used by programs to display graphics and text on the screen. Basically an *object-oriented* graphical language, QuickDraw performs some of the same kinds of functions as *PostScript* but is much less powerful. A *PICT* graphic file is really just a set of QuickDraw commands that cause the image to be drawn on the screen.

QuickDraw printer   Clever phrase coined by Apple to make a drawback sound like an advantage. A "QuickDraw printer" isn't a printer that has *QuickDraw*—QuickDraw is in the Mac, not in the printer—it's simply a printer that doesn't have *PostScript*. It's really a brain-dead machine, but calling it a "QuickDraw printer" makes it sound as though it has a nifty feature, doesn't it?

Q

QuicKeys A widely used *macro* utility from CE
Software, this lets you assign a whole set of
actions—mouse clicks, drags, typing, and so
forth—to a single keystroke. For example, you
could set up a QuicKeys macro so that when you pressed
Shift-Command-S, QuicKeys would type "Sincerely yours,
Theophilus Q. Hasenpfeffer, PhD", thereby saving you a
lot of typing! Macros are handy for automating repetitive
chores, and QuicKeys is the most reliable macro program around.

QuickTime A way of playing back animated
movies or digitized video—with synchronized
sound—on any Mac that has a 68020 *microprocessor* or better. The tricky part is to make
the movie play back at the right speed,
whether it's running on an old, slow Mac II or a fast new
Quadra, and QuickTime manages this nicely by adjusting
its playback rate to suit the capability of your Mac's
processor. On a slower machine it may show you only
every third frame of the movie, while on a fast Mac it'll play
every frame.

QuickTime uses built-in video compression to reduce the
size of its movie files, but still they tend to be rather large:
hundreds of K for just a few seconds of playback time. QT
also lets other graphics applications use its built-in *JPEG*
compression to save space on still images saved in *PICT*
format. What is QuickTime exactly? It's simply an *extension* that must be placed in your *System Folder* in order to
work its magic.

QWERTY (kwerty) Something you probably take for
granted is the arrangement of your keyboard. If you're in
the US, most likely the first row of letters starts off
"qwerty"—hence the name. This arrangement dates back
to the original Sholes typewriter of the late nineteenth
century, whose mechanism sometimes jammed when a
fast typist used it. The QWERTY keyboard was actually
designed to slow down these speed-demon typists so the
typewriter wouldn't jam. Although the need has long since
passed, the deliberately inefficient QWERTY layout is still

with us a hundred years later. There is an alternative, though: the Dvorak keyboard layout, designed for speedy typing. If you want to try it, most *BBSs* and *information services* like *AOL* carry *public-domain* utilities that can reprogram your Mac keyboard to Dvorak format.

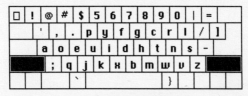

The QWERTY layout

Q

Rr

radio button An on-screen button that's one of a group of mutually exclusive choices; like the buttons on your car radio, where you can choose only one station at a time.

Alignment:
- ○ Tops
- ◉ Centers
- ○ Bottoms

radiosity A way of *rendering*, which means depicting realistic shadows and reflections on a simulated 3D object. Radiosity is the most advanced method now in use; it takes into effect not only the simulated objects but also atmospheric effects like dust and fog, allowing extremely realistic depictions. Naturally, it also takes the longest to compute! Other rendering methods include *Phong* and *Gouraud shading*.

rag right See *ragged right*.

ragged right Said of text that's set with a flush left margin and a "ragged" right margin. Studies have shown that ragged right text is slightly easier to read than fully *justified* text, which is flush on both margins.

RAM Random Access Memory. Computer memory in the form of integrated circuit *chips* that remember their contents only as long as the computer is turned on. Information can be written to or read from RAM in billionths of a second, which is about ten thousand times faster than a hard disk or floppy disk can do it.

RAM disk Since hard disks are a thousand times slower than RAM (memory), one way of speeding up a program that uses the disk drive frequently is to set up an area in RAM that pretends to be a disk drive but is much, much faster. Of course, you have to have RAM to spare, but that's not hard at today's prices. Only one problem with this little trick: unlike a real disk, a RAM disk forgets as soon as power is lost. So if your program goes happily along saving to what it thinks is a disk file (but is really a

R

RAM disk) and then there's a sudden power glitch, well—all that stuff is gone! It's up to you: you can choose speed or security. Since most folks choose security, RAM disks are not too popular.

raster A grid of horizontal lines—for example, the horizontal scan lines that make up a TV picture, or the rows of tiny black dots that make up a printed page. Basically, "raster" is just another word for a displayed *bitmap*.

rasterize To convert to a *raster*. That was obvious, wasn't it? Okay, so what does it really mean? Well, let's take a character in a typical *PostScript* typeface. If you read about PostScript, you know that each character is just a set of *Bézier curves*. But a video display is not made of curves; it's a regular array of square pixels—a raster. Ditto a printout on paper: it's a grid of black dots.

There has to be a way to get from the curves of the PostScript version to the screen raster or the printed bitmap. This is the job of a rasterizer, a piece of software built into every PostScript interpreter (and into *ATM* and *TrueType* software). It takes the curves and translates them into an equivalent pattern of dots on the screen or on paper.

ray tracing A way of *rendering*, which means depicting realistic shadows and reflections in a simulated 3D scene. It works by starting at the eye of an imaginary spectator and tracing each ray of light entering that eye backward to its origin. Since the light ray may bounce from object to object or be refracted as it passes through clear objects, the path can be pretty complicated—and there are a lot of rays! As you can imagine, this is very time-consuming; it can take hours to do even on a fast Mac.

Read Me The common name for a text file that tells you the latest on a program you've just bought. Typically, you'll find a Read Me File (usually in *TeachText* format) on one of the floppies that comes with a new software package; it covers developments that occurred too late to make it into the printed documentation. Be sure to read it!

read-only   A disk or file that can't be altered—
you can read it but not write to it. You can
make a floppy disk read-only by sliding its
write-protect tab to the open position; you can
make a file read-only by clicking on the *locked* check box in
its Get Info dialog box.

read/write head   The part of a disk drive that records and
plays back information. It has a tiny, delicate coil whose
electromagnetic field rearranges the magnetic particles on
a disk in order to write a file. When it's time to read the file
back, the read/write head acts as a pickup, sensing the
magnetic fields on the spinning disk and converting them
to electrical signals.

reboot   To restart your computer. Why "reboot"? See *boot*
for the explanation, a bit of historical trivia.

rebuild the desktop   The Finder stores information
about all the files on a disk in an invisible file called the
*desktop.*It's sort of like the table of contents in a book:
when you need to find something, you can look it up in the
table of contents. But sometimes the desktop file gets
damaged—or worse, infected by a *virus* like *WDEF*. Fortunately, when that happens, there's an easy fix: the
Finder can rebuild the desktop file by looking at the
contents of the disk and making a brand-new desktop. To
force the Finder to do this, just hold down the *Option* and
Command keys while starting up (for your hard disk) or
while inserting a floppy disk. You should do this routinely
every month or two just to keep your desktop file clean.
One caution: any comment you've typed into a file's *Get
Info* box will be lost when you rebuild the desktop. This,
of course, makes Get Info comments effectively worthless
in the long run. Stupid? Yes, but that's the way Apple
programmed it.

record   A collection of related information in a *database*.
Imagine a typical customer database. Each customer has
a record; each record contains several *fields,* such as
name, address, phone number, account balance, and so
on. Taken together, the related fields make up a record of

all you know about that particular customer. Think of a record as a 3" x 5" file card and the fields as the lines of information on the card.

refresh rate   The speed at which a video monitor redraws its screen. If the rate is slow—say, below 65 Hz (65 times per second)—you may notice annoying flicker. Most good monitors have a 70–75 Hz or better refresh rate.

relational   Said of a *database* management program, this means that it is able to access several data files at once (for example, a customer list and a list of orders) and prepare reports based on related information contained in them.

render   To depict realistic-looking surfaces, shadows, and reflections on a simulated three-dimensional object. A renderer is a program that takes a mathematical model of 3D objects (created in another program) and converts it into a 2D *bitmapped* image of those objects as viewed from a given vantage point. This can be done in a variety of ways (see *Gouraud shading*, *Phong shading*, *radiosity*, and *ray tracing* for some specifics), but rendering generally requires lots of computer power and lots of time. A typical 3D scene may take hours to render, even on a fast Mac Quadra. For this reason, folks who are using these 3D programs generally work with simplified "wireframe" models on screen and leave rendering until the end.

RenderMan   A program from the well-known graphics company Pixar, RenderMan *renders* 3D scenes and objects—that is, it takes a geometric, mathematical description created in another program and creates a strikingly realistic visual depiction of it in the screen, drawing shadows, reflections, surface textures, and so forth. Perhaps the most sophisticated of the many available renderers, RenderMan has hopes of becoming an industry standard.

reorg   (REE ORG) An Apple ritual enacted at least once a year: everybody gets to play musical chairs as the company rearranges its structure completely, demoralizing employees and confusing customers. Reorgs are the reason that your contact in Tech Support won't be there next time you call; she'll have been shipped to Claris to work on marketing. It's hard to form stable working relationships with a company that reshuffles its personnel so frequently, and Apple's own projects are disrupted as employees are arbitrarily reassigned elsewhere. Apple calls this "staying flexible." Apple employees call it things I can't print here.

ResEdit (REZ EH DIT) Resource Editor. A program available from Apple that can be used to customize things like menus, dialog boxes, fonts, icons, desk accessories, and much more—even if you're not a programmer! This ability to modify *resources* is one of the most powerful features of the Mac. For example, a person with no programming knowledge can take a program and convert it to Portuguese—all its menus, dialog boxes, alerts, and text. This is unheard of in the *DOS* world, or indeed on any other computer.

ResEdit is wonderful fun if you like to take things apart to see what makes them tick—for example, you can open a commercial program with it and browse through all the obscure error messages you'd never ordinarily see. You may even find hidden features in your favorite program! A common use for ResEdit is to add keyboard shortcuts to program menus so that you can choose commands without using the mouse. Just be careful—ResEdit can do permanent damage. Use it only if you know what you're doing, and never on original files!

reset switch A small piece of plastic with a triangle on it, used as a last resort when software *freezes*. It comes in various shapes and locations depending on what model you have. On older Macs (the Plus and SE), it's on the left side near the back. On Macs like the II, IIx, and IIfx it's on the right side near the back. On compact Macs like the IIcx and IIci, it's on the front at the lower left. The next time a program *freezes*, hit the reset switch (the one with the little triangle). This is better than turning off the power, which is hard on your Mac's power supply if you do it too often.

resize box See *size box.*

resolution The number of dots per inch (dpi) on the screen or on paper. For example, the standard Macintosh screen display has a resolution of 72 dpi, the ImageWriter II has a resolution of 144 dpi, and the LaserWriters have a resolution of 300 dpi.

resource   One of a variety of building blocks used in all Macintosh programs. Things like windows, menus, *alert* and *dialog* boxes, *fonts,* and much more are all included in a typical program. What looks like one file to the user is actually a collection of these separate modules, plus program instructions *("code"),* which are themselves a resource. The advantage of this scheme, which is unique to the Macintosh, is that the pieces can be cut, copied, pasted, and edited quite easily, even if you didn't write the original program. To do this, you use the utility program *ResEdit.*

resource fork   Okay, it's pretty esoteric, but you just might run into this phrase sometime. It refers to the part of a Macintosh file that contains its *resources* 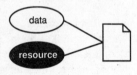 (for example, icons, menus, dialogs, code, and so forth), as opposed to the file's *data fork* (for example, the text in a MacWrite document). A file may have either a data fork, a resource fork, or both. Typically, applications always have resources and may also have data; documents always have data and may also have resources. Normally, you won't ever see the two forks as separate entities, but they're there behind the scenes.

Restart   A *Finder* command equivalent to doing a shutdown, followed immediately by a startup. You'll need to do this, for example, after making changes to settings in some control panels (such as Memory), because the changes won't take effect until you restart.

RGB   Red/Green/Blue. Describes video equipment that accepts separate red, green, and blue input signals. All color video displays use a combination of red, green, and blue light-emitting dots or stripes to create the complete spectrum of colors we can see. However, the video (picture) signal that's sent to the display can be encoded in one of several ways.

In VCRs and inexpensive computers (such as the Amiga), all the information is combined into one signal, called *composite video*, which can be sent over a single pair of wires. Circuitry inside the video display takes this composite signal apart and sends its red, green, and blue components to the corresponding guns in the picture tube.

A better way of doing things, used in high-quality displays like the Mac II's, is to send the red, green, and blue signals separately; this is known as RGB. This makes cables and connectors a bit more complicated, but it yields far better picture quality thanks to its increased sharpness and purer colors. A standard Apple color monitor can display about four times as many *pixels,* or picture dots, as a regular TV (by the way, this is why you can't save money by using your TV as a Mac monitor). Even today's most expensive TV sets lack the *resolution* to show Macintosh graphics sharply.

RIB RenderMan Interface Bytestream. A standard format for 3D model files intended for *rendering* by *RenderMan.* Many programs can export RIB files—it's pretty much a standard for sophisticated 3D documents.

RIFF (RIFF) Raster Image File Format. A way of storing *bitmapped* graphic images. Like *TIFF,* it's used mostly for *scanned* images. Only a few Mac programs (such as Digital Darkroom and ImageStudio) use RIFF format; TIFF is far more common.

RIP (RIP) Raster Image Processor. A special-purpose computer that converts *PostScript's* mathematical curves into a bitmap suitable for printing. Technically, every PostScript printer has one of these, but this term usually refers to a separate box that drives a high-resolution *imagesetter* like a *Linotronic.*

RISC (RISK) Reduced Instruction Set Computing. A style of *microprocessor* design which favors a small, simple set of instructions that can be executed very fast. Many current microprocessors, such as the Mac's 68000 series, are CISC (Complex Instruction Set Computing) devices. Their large variety of instructions makes life easier for

R

programmers, but slows down execution compared to the simpler, more efficient RISC chips. Because of the speed advantage of RISC designs, the next generation of personal computers from Apple, IBM and others will be based on RISC chips.

RJ-11 The little cube of clear plastic on the end of a telephone wire—a "modular plug" in phone company jargon—is called an RJ-11 connector. These handy crimp-on connectors are used for many things besides telephones. For example, the original Macs had keyboard cables with RJ-11 connectors, and they're also widely used in *AppleTalk* networking schemes such as *PhoneNet*.

ROM (ROM) Read Only Memory. Permanent computer memory in the form of integrated circuit *chips* that are programmed at the factory and whose contents cannot be changed. ROM chips are used to store parts of the Mac's *operating system* so that it will have essential programs available as soon as power is turned on. Like *RAM* chips, ROMs are very fast.

root directory The first window you see when you double-click the icon of a disk on the *desktop*. The folders-within-folders directory structure of the Mac can be thought of as a tree with the root directory at its lowest level—all the other directories are attached to the root, like branches of a tree.

ROTFLOL Rolling On The Floor Laughing Out Loud. *Telecommunications* shorthand; you'll often see this in *electronic mail* messages.

router A box that connects two or more network *zones* together, routing electronic messages between them. Why not just put everybody on one huge network instead? Because if ten or twenty people are simultaneously trying to send mail, the network bogs down and everyone spends a lot of time waiting. Breaking up the network into several zones means that the number of users in any one zone is small enough not to overload it, and they can still send messages to users in other zones through the router.

RSN Real Soon Now. What the software publishers always say about long-overdue program updates: "It'll be in the stores Real Soon Now!" Programs like this are called *vaporware.*

RS-232 A commonly-used standard for sending data through a cable in *serial* form. The standard specifies voltage levels and pin assignments on a D-shaped connector called a DB-25 (although RS-232 is a fairly loose standard, and has been implemented on a variety of nonstandard connectors). In the Mac world, RS-232 is used mainly to communicate with modems.

RTF Rich Text Format. A format for text files, originated by Microsoft. It stores not only the text itself, but things like what fonts and styles were used. Most word processors and page layout programs can work with RTF files.

RTFM Read The Friggin' Manual! A phrase you may hear a tech support person mutter under her breath as she tries to be polite with a caller who wants to know how to do something that's clearly explained on page 7 of the owner's manual (which, true to Mac tradition, the caller hasn't read).

rule 1) A thin horizontal or vertical line used to separate sections of text in a publication like a book or newspaper.

2) A recommended way of writing programs. Apple sets forth many rules in the *Inside Macintosh* books; programmers who don't follow them tend to produce code that breaks (crashes) whenever anything about the Mac *operating system* changes even slightly. Since Apple updates the system software at least once a year, it pays to follow the rules if you don't want to have to issue frequent bug-fix updates. (See *Microsoft.)* Then again, Apple doesn't always follow its own rules, as owners of the Apple 8•24GC video card can testify!

R

Ss

Sad Mac   A frowning Mac face that appears
on startup when you have (usually) serious
hardware problems (like improperly installed
memory) with older Macs. Underneath the `0F0064`
face is a set of codes that can be deciphered
(if you have an Official Apple Technician Secret Decoder
Ring) to tell you what has gone wrong. Missing or bad *boot
blocks* on a disk can also cause this to appear. Newer Macs
have augmented the Sad Mac with a typical too-cute-for-
its-own-good Apple gimmick: the *Chimes of Doom*. This
arpeggiated chord (or chords) is a code also, but only a
musician with perfect pitch can figure out what it means!

SANE (SANE)   Standard Apple Numerics Environment.
When a Mac program needs to do calculations, it doesn't
have to have its own *algorithms*—it can simply make calls
to the number-crunching functions that Apple has thought-
fully built into every Mac. These built-in SANE routines
can do all the common operations (addition, division,
square root calculation, and so forth) to very high numeric
precision.

However, SANE takes relatively long to arrive at its oh-so-
precise answers, when in some cases a quicker, rougher
calculation would be just as good. Some companies offer
software *extensions* that bypass the SANE routines in
favor of faster, lower-precision math routines of their own.
With this software, you can choose between speed and
accuracy.

sans-serif   A typeface or *font* that lacks *serifs*, the
crosswise end strokes on most letters. ("Sans" is
French for "without.") Commonly used sans-serif
fonts are Helvetica and Avant Garde. Sans-serif fonts are
fine at large sizes, but the lack of the distinguishing serifs
makes them harder to read at small sizes (under 12 points)
than serif fonts, so they're less than ideal for body text. But
that's just a rule of thumb, so feel free to experiment!

scalable font 1) Synonymous with *outline font*.

2) For *DOS* users, a hot new technological breakthrough.

3) For Mac users, something we've all taken for granted since PostScript was introduced in 1985.

scanner A handy gadget that translates a paper document into an image file in your computer. It works just like the input half of a *fax* machine. First you run a special program that controls the scanner, then you put your document on it (or feed it through a slot on some models). It whirs and hums for a while, then a ragged-looking version of the document appears on your screen. You can use this image (which is a *bitmap*, similar to a giant MacPaint file) as a graphic, or run an optical character recognition *(OCR)* program to "read" the text information from it.

Scitex A series of large, very expensive (hundreds of thousands of bucks), very powerful image-processing systems used in the publishing business to retouch photographs and perform other graphics chores. The Mac (combined with Adobe's Photoshop program) is slowly encroaching on its territory, but the Scitex's special-purpose hardware is still faster than the hottest Macs currently available. The handwriting is clearly visible on the wall, however; ten years from now, dedicated photo-retouching systems like Scitex's will be where dedicated typesetting systems are now—well on their way to museum-piece status.

Scrapbook A handy application (or *desk accessory* on older Macs) that can store frequently used graphics, text, or other things (including *QuickTime* movies). The Scrapbook can hold the basic

Scrapbook File

Mac data formats: *PICT* graphics, QuickTime movies, sounds, and text. That means, among other things, that PostScript graphics lose their high-quality characteristics, and text loses its font, size, and style information when stored in the Scrapbook.

screen 1) That light-up glass thingie on your Mac—the one you spend so many hours staring at.

2) A graphic-arts term that describes the grid of dots into which a photograph is broken in order to turn it into a *halftone*. Remember, most printers have only one color of ink: black. In order to simulate the grays in a photo, you use a lot of tiny black dots, some larger than others. Viewed from a distance, this fools the eye into thinking it sees gray.

To turn a *grayscale* photo into a halftone, printers originally used a fine mesh screen to break the picture into dots. The finer the screen, the smoother the resulting image. Screens are specified in lines per inch *(lpi)*. Typical newspaper photos may be printed with 80–100 lpi screens; magazines can go as high as 200 lpi; and "coffee table" art books may run as high as 300 lpi.

screen dump A graphics file (usually MacPaint or *PICT* format) containing an image of what was on the screen when the dump was performed. Such a file can be created by holding down the Shift and Command keys and pressing 3. With System 7, this creates a color PICT file called "Picture 1" (subsequent dumps will be named "Picture 2," and so on). With older versions of the operating system, you'll get black and white *MacPaint* files starting with "Screen 0".

screen font A low-resolution *bitmapped* font used to display characters on the screen (as opposed to a *PostScript* font, which is used to print them on paper). **Script Fonts**

screen refresh The time it takes to redraw the Mac's video screen from top to bottom. Refresh rates vary between 60 and 90 *Hz* (times per second). The faster the refresh rate, the less likely you are to be annoyed by flicker.

screen saver A program, like After Dark or Pyro, that automatically darkens the screen after a period of inactivity in order to save the picture tube from phosphor "burn-in" caused by having the same image on the screen for a long time. Typically, the screen saver is an extension (startup document) or control panel that lives in your *System Folder*. If about ten minutes go by without any keyboard or mouse activity, the screen saver darkens the screen and displays a small, randomly moving pattern or icon to let you know the machine's still on. Moving the mouse or hitting any key brings back the normal screen display.

script This is really just another word for a *program*, but companies have been using it lately when they're afraid of scaring off users who don't think of themselves as programmers. Scripting capabilities can be found in programs like *HyperCard*, PageMaker, and MicroPhone, where scripts can be used to automate many program functions.

scroll bar An area at the edge of a window, used as a control for moving through the document in the window. For example, a window showing you a report you're working on may let you see only a few paragraphs at a time. Using the scroll bar, you can move the document up or down under the window to let you see and work on other parts of your text. There are three ways to use a scroll bar: 1) press on the arrow buttons for continuous scrolling; 2) click in the gray area to scroll one windowful at a time; and 3) drag the little box (sometimes called the *thumb*) to go directly to a desired part of the document.

SCSI (scuzzy) Small Computer Systems Interface. A hardware and software standard for connecting things like hard disks or scanners to the Mac; SCSI is a fast way to move large amounts of data from one device to another. Originally developed by hard disk maker Shugart Associates and called Shugart Associates Systems Interface (SASI), it later became an industry standard and changed its name to SCSI. The Mac Plus was the first home computer with a SCSI interface (although Apple's version of SCSI is not quite the industry standard).

Sculley, John Former president of Pepsico, he brought his extensive experience at selling flavored sugar water into the computer business. Sculley was recruited to Apple in the mid-eighties at a time when the company was undergoing rapid expansion and needed more professional management than founders Steve *Wozniak* and Steve *Jobs* could provide. To their surprise and dismay, both Steves were soon eased out of their own company and Sculley assumed control. While the pace of technological innovation has slowed somewhat during his regime, Sculley can take credit for making Apple listen harder to its customers and to the realities of the marketplace, resulting in much less expensive Macs.

SECAM (SEE KAM) Système Electronique pour Couleur Avec Mémoire. A standard for transmitting television signals that's used in France, eastern Europe, and parts of the middle east. (Other television systems are the US *NTSC* and British *PAL* standards.) SECAM has better color fidelity and 20 percent higher vertical resolution than NTSC. SECAM signals (from broadcasts, videotapes, or videodiscs) cannot be displayed by US TV sets.

sector An area on a disk (either a *hard disk* or *floppy disk)*; part of a *track*. Sector size can range from 512 *bytes* (on a floppy) to several thousand bytes (on hard disks). The Mac's *operating system* always writes or reads full sectors; it cannot deal with parts of sectors. For example, saving a 513-byte file to a floppy takes up two 512-byte sectors, even though the second one contains only one byte of useful data. This may seem wasteful of disk space (and it is), but operations would slow to a crawl if the computer had to write to the disk byte by byte instead of sector by sector. Thus, sector size is a compromise between access speed and efficient use of disk space.

seek time The time it takes to position the read/write heads of a *disk drive* to a particular *track*. Obviously, the faster it can do this, the faster you're going to be able to get your work done.

select To mark something in or-   this is ■selected■ text
der to perform some operation
on it—for example, to *highlight* text so that you can make
it bold, or to click on a file's icon so that you can drag it to
the *Trash*.

separate To produce separate master documents *(cam-era-ready copy)* for each of several colors you intend to
print. Since a printing press can normally print only one
color at a time, a separate printing plate has to be made for
each color. For example, *process color* work requires four
plates: one each for cyan, magenta, yellow, and black.
Software like Adobe Separator or Aldus PrePrint is used to
convert a full-color computer graphic into the four masters
needed.

serial A way of connecting a printer or *modem* to a Mac in
which information is sent one *bit* at a time. Mac printers
are almost always connected this way (except for the
obsolete *LaserWriter IISC*). IBM computers and *clones,* on
the other hand, generally use a *parallel* interface for
printing, so they won't work with most printers made for
Macintoshes and vice versa. Unlike printers, modems are
always connected with a serial interface, so they'll work
with either type of computer (except for internal modems,
which go inside the computer).

serif A crosswise stroke at the end of a letter.   T
Commonly used serif fonts include Bookman,
New Century Schoolbook, and Times (actually
Times New Roman, but abbreviated for the sake of smaller
menus to "Times"). A typeface with no serifs is called a
sans-serif face.

server A computer with a large hard disk, connected by a
local area *network (LAN)* such as *AppleTalk* to a number
of other computers. The users of the computers connected
to the server can use it just as if it were another hard disk
on their own Macs.

service bureau A company that has expensive equipment you can't afford but lets you use it (for a fee). Usually
that means *imagesetters* (like *Linotronics),* slide imaging

devices, large computer-driven vinyl sign cutters, and so on. Typically, it works like this: you create documents on your Mac with PageMaker or Quark *Xpress* and print proofs on your *LaserWriter* at 300 dots per inch. Then you take the files to a service bureau, where they print out the documents on their *Lino* at 1270 dpi or higher. You can expect to pay about $6 to $8 a page for this service.

sexy When you can't wait to get your hands on it; when you want it so badly that you think about it all the time, maybe even dream about it—that's sexy! Sexiness can lie in the way a product looks, in what it does, or both. Applies to hardware (full-color dye-sublimation printers are currently very sexy) and software (Fractal Design's Painter). Of course, it's a matter of taste—there's probably someone somewhere who thinks *TeachText* is sexy!

shareware Commercial software on the honor system. Programmers create software and distribute it through networks like *AOL* and user group libraries; the software usually carries a notice that says something like, "Copy this and share it with anyone you like. Try it yourself for up to 30 days; if you like it, please send me $15." Since there's no distribution or advertising overhead, shareware prices are extremely low for what you get. The better shareware authors support and enhance their programs on an ongoing basis, so registered users are eligible for free (or at-cost) upgrades. Unfortunately, few people (maybe two or three in a hundred) pay for the shareware they use, so shareware authors don't get much money. That's too bad, because there are many shareware programs that are actually better than commercial software—and at far cheaper prices!

Sharing Setup A control panel that lets you start and stop *Personal File Sharing*, a System 7 feature that lets you share documents or programs with other Macs on a *network*. The Sharing Setup control panel lets you determine just what you'll make available to other users, and who can access it.

shift-click A way of selecting more than one item at a time (Apple calls this "extended selection"). For example, hold down the Shift key while clicking on several files to select them, then drag them all to another disk to copy them. If you're working with text, you can usually click at the beginning of a document or list and then shift-click at the end to select everything in between.

SIG (SIG) Special Interest Group. A subdivision of a computer organization or *user group*. The SIGs usually meet separately to discuss their own special areas of interest.

SIMM (SIM) Single Inline Memory Module. A type of *RAM* (memory); it's a little thing about the size of a stick of chewing gum, usually with eight or nine lumps on it (these are RAM *chips*), that plugs into a socket inside your Mac. Since SIMMs come in different varieties and speeds, it's very important to make sure you get the right kind for your Mac.

Very early Macs (the Mac 128, Mac 512, and Mac 512Ke) and some Mac portables can't use SIMMs for memory expansion, but you can increase RAM in these machines with add-on boards from companies like Dove.

.sit (SIT) Often appended to the name of a file that has been compressed with the utility program *StuffIt*—for example, "Hippopotamus collection.sit".

Archive.sit

size box The little square in the lower right corner of a window; dragging it lets you change the window's size. And here's a little-known trick: if you have an older program that won't let you enlarge its window to fill your new large display, try holding down the Option key while dragging the size box. If you're in luck, this will let you stretch the window beyond its former limits! It doesn't always work, but it's worth a try.

slot A long, skinny connector inside your computer; it's there so you can plug in accessory *boards* that give your Mac more speed, memory, or other added capabilities. Different Macs have different kinds of slots; be careful that the board you plug in matches the computer it's going into or you could cause expensive damage. Many Macs (like the IIci and Quadra models) have *NuBus* slots; boards for these are freely interchangeable.

small caps Generally, characters you type when holding down the Shift key (capital or uppercase letters) have completely different shapes than unshifted characters (lowercase letters). When you use small caps, characters that would normally be lowercase letters look just like capital letters, only smaller. (LIKE THIS, IN OTHER WORDS.) Most *word processors* and *page layout programs* can create small caps simply by scaling down the full-sized capitals, but this approach yields characters with unnaturally skinny *stems*. To remedy this, type vendors like *Adobe* offer families of type that include specially designed small caps, with stem weights that match the corresponding lower-case letters. (By the way, pronunciations in this dictionary are set in small caps.)

smart quotes The sort of quotation marks you see in books and magazines: curly (""), and facing in opposite directions—not straight up like the dumb ("") quotes on a typewriter. (Take a good look at those two pairs of quotes to see the difference!) Some programs automatically substitute smart quotes (and apostrophes) for dumb ones, but you can always get them by holding down Option while you type [(for ") and Shift-Option-[(for "). Similarly, Option-] gets you ' and Shift-Option-] gets you '.

S

smilies Little faces turned sidewise; used in *electronic mail (email)* messages to convey nuances of feelings that would otherwise be lost in cold print. For example, :) is a smiling face and ;) is a winking one. : (, of course, is a frown. This may all seem pretty silly, but it's surprisingly easy to be misunderstood in an email message—to mean something tongue-in-cheek, but have it interpreted as being dead serious. A wink ;) or a smile :) can go a long way toward avoiding painful misunderstandings—the kind that can escalate into *flame* wars. Speaking of tongues, by the way, : **P** means sticking out your tongue at someone.

SMPTE time code (SIMP TEE) Society of Motion Picture and Television Engineers. A special timing code used by video professionals to help in editing film, videotape, and soundtracks. SMPTE code identifies the hour, minute, second, and frame of each moment in a film or video. Consumer video equipment doesn't use SMPTE code—yet—but the price of professional VCRs and cameras that do is slowly edging downward. For really precise editing, it's indispensable.

sneakernet Sometimes the best network is no network: no expensive cards, cumbersome wiring, complex data protocols, network administrators, passwords, and so forth. So how do you get a file to your coworker in the office down the hall? Save it on a floppy, then let your sneakers carry you, and it, down the hall. In short—sneakernet!

soft hyphen A hyphen (also called a "discretionary hyphen") that remains invisible until the word containing it gets close to the end of a line, at which point the word breaks at the soft hyphen. It's a way for you to tell a program, "If you have to break this word, break it here." Not all programs let you do this, but those that do (such as PageMaker) generally recognize Option-hyphen as a soft hyphen. By contrast, a *hard hyphen* (the usual kind) is always visible.

soft return In some word processors and page layout programs, this forces the text entry point down to the beginning of the next line but does not begin a new paragraph. (This is sometimes called a line break.) By contrast, the normal return you get when you press the return key is a *hard return*. The hard return forces the text entry point down to the beginning of the next line and begins a new paragraph, so if you have chosen an *indent* or extra space between paragraphs, those will be inserted automatically.

software The lists of instructions that make a computer do useful work. Think of computer *hardware* as being like a cook. The software is the recipe that tells the cook how to make Baked Alaska and the data are the ingredients that go into the finished dish.

Sound A *control panel* that lets you adjust the volume of your Mac's speaker and choose what sound will be used as a system beep in case of errors. How do the sounds get into the control panel's list? Well, if you have a sound on the *Clipboard* and the Sound control panel is open, you can paste the sound into the list and use it as a beep sound. And if you have a Mac with a mike (such as an LC or IIsi), you can record sounds from the microphone directly into the Sound control panel.

Speaker
Volume

7 -
6 -
5 -
4 -
3 -
2 -
1 -
0 -

spell checker 1) Something used by witches, wizards and warlocks to ensure the correctness of their magical spells.

2) A phrase often misused by those who are in desperate need of a good spelling checker. Remember: magicians need to check spells. The rest of us need to check spelling. Got it? Okay, I promise I'll stop lecturing now.

spool Simultaneous Peripheral Operation On Line (an old IBM acronym). To print a document while simultaneously working on something else; a simple form of *multitasking*. Software that does this is called a "spooler."

spooler Something that *spools*. But I bet you already figured that out, huh?

spot color Simple solid colors used as decoration in a printed document—like a red line at the top of each section of a book, or a blue initial cap in each paragraph— as opposed to full-color photos and complex multicolored illustrations.

S

spreadsheet A program that simulates an accountant's worksheet, typically dividing the screen into rows and columns of cells, each of which can contain a number (such as the current balance for one account), a label (such as "Balances"), or a formula (such as the sum of all current balances in this column). The formulas mean that the values in various cells affect each other. If you change, for example, one of the account balances, the grand total is recalculated and displayed in its cell. The most popular Mac spreadsheet is Microsoft's Excel.

SQL Structured Query Language. A computer language whose special purpose is to search for information in large *databases*. If you need to see all the customer records from Minnesota that are more than two months overdue but whose balances do not exceed $5,000, you can create an SQL query to do it.

stack A *HyperCard* "document," a stack is not exactly a document in the sense we normally use that term. Depending on how it was put together, it can be very like a program, similar to a database file, or some mixture of the two. Confusing? Well, that's the flexibility of HyperCard for you. Since it can do almost anything (as long as you're not in a hurry), it's tough to get a handle on exactly what it is.

standalone Able to run by itself, without help from any other programs. For example, a *BASIC* program is not a standalone program because it must have a BASIC interpreter in order to run; the same is true of *HyperCard stacks* (although SuperCard can turn a HyperCard stack into a standalone SuperCard application). An application such as MacWrite is a standalone program; you can double-click it and it runs without needing any other files to be present.

startup disk A *floppy* or *hard disk* that contains a *System Folder*—in other words, a disk that has what it takes to get your Mac going when you turn on the power.

Startup Disk A *control panel* that lets you choose which of several *SCSI hard disks* will be used as the startup disk when you turn on your Mac. (The disk you choose must have a *System Folder* on it.)

Startup Items A special folder inside your *System Folder*. Under System 7, any program put into this folder automatically runs as soon as your Mac starts up. For example, if the first thing you always do is to connect to the *America Online* network and check your mail, you might put the AOL application into the Startup Items folder.

static RAM Memory that retains its data as long as power is applied; as long as it has juice, it just sits there and remembers for you. That takes very little power, so SRAM is often used in portable computers. Unfortunately, it's relatively expensive. By contrast, dynamic RAM *(DRAM)* is inexpensive, but needs to be constantly exercised in order to remember—sort of like the French you learned in high school. That takes a lot more power than static RAM.

stationery Traditionally, stationery is a mostly blank piece of paper with some information preprinted on it— your address and phone number, usually. Similarly, computer stationery is a mostly blank electronic document with some things preset—font, size, style, maybe even your name and address typed in. When you open a stationery document, the original is left untouched; the Mac creates a copy called "Untitled" for you to work on— sort of like tearing off a piece of paper from a pad. You can fill it in, name it, and save or print it.

S

You can make any document into stationery if you're running *System 7:* just click its icon once to select it, then Get Info (from the File menu) and click in the document's Stationery check box. It's a handy way to make "tear-off pads" of your letterhead, business forms, and so on.

stem A vertical stroke in a letter or number.

stop bit When sending data over a *serial* connection (for example, via *modem*), your computer follows certain rules. Typically, it sends eight data bits, followed by a *parity* bit (for error checking), then comes a stop bit, which tells the computer on the other end, "Hey, that's the end of this byte!" At very slow speeds, two stop bits may be required.

string A collection of alphabetic characters, a string can be anything from a single letter to a chapter in a book. It's called a string because, regardless of how it's shown on the screen, it's stored as a linear group of characters, like pearls on a string.

stuffed file A file that has been compressed with *StuffIt*. You can usually recognize one by the suffix .sit appended to its filename.

StuffIt A clever *shareware* program that's able to compress files by removing redundant information, then reconstitute them when needed. The "unstuffed" files are exactly the same as the originals—no data is lost. Stuffed files can be as little as half the size of the originals, though sixty to eighty percent is more typical. As a result, they take up less space and require less time to upload to or download from a Bulletin Board System (*BBS*) or *network*, thus saving money. Most files on Mac BBSs and networks (like *AOL*) are in StuffIt form. StuffIt can also combine several related files into one, allowing you to bundle together a program and its documentation. By convention, stuffed files usually have .sit added to their filenames, as for example "MyProgram.sit."

styles 1) Variations on a typeface, such as bold, italic, and outline.

2) A powerful feature of many *word processors* and *page layout programs* that lets you assign a whole set of characteristics to a block of text with a single command. For example, you can define a style called "Head" that has Avant Garde bold type, set at 24 *points* on 30-point *leading*, centered on the page, with 6 *picas* of space following each return. Then you can select a line of text, choose "Head" from your style menu—and all those attributes are instantly applied, saving you a heck of a lot of mousing and menu-pulling. From now on, all you need to do is select the text of each headline and assign the proper style.

But there's more. Suppose you use the Head style for every headline in your newsletter. Later on, you decide that you'd prefer Futura to Avant Garde. All you have to do is go into the style's definition and change the font, and presto! All the headlines throughout your document are changed automatically. Needless to say, styles are a tremendous time-saver.

StyleWriter A relatively inexpensive but unbelievably slow *inkjet* printer made by Apple. Its print quality is excellent—about equal to a *LaserWriter*—if you don't mind waiting two to four minutes per page! A bargain for those with lots of time on their hands.

submenu A menu that pops out from the side of a main menu item to provide additional choices. When you see a small right-pointing triangle next to a menu item,

you know that item has a submenu just waiting to pop out. (Also called a *hierarchical* menu.)

subscribe To link a document created with one program to a document created with another (available only in *System 7*). A section of the first document (for example, a business chart from a spreadsheet) is *published,* creating a separate *edition* file on your disk. The second document—which might be an annual report that includes the chart—subscribes to the edition. When you change the chart, you can update the edition, which can in turn automatically update the annual report.

suitcase file A file containing *fonts* or *desk accessories,* with an *icon* in the shape of a suitcase. In order to use them, you must copy the contents of a suitcase into your *System* file (itself a suitcase file), unless you have the commercial utility program *Suitcase,* which can use the contents of suitcase files without any need for installation.

Display fonts

Suitcase II A widely used commercial *extension* that lets you use the *fonts* and *desk accessories (DAs)* contained in *suitcase files* without permanently installing them in the usual way. That's handy because it means you can quickly install a seldom-used font in order to do a special job, then just as quickly remove it when you're done. Suitcase also lets your font menu show the actual fonts (not just their names) and does other useful things. There's just one problem with this wonderful program: its name. If you've spent as much time as I have telling new Mac users over the phone, "Now use Suitcase to open the suitcase—that is, use the Suitcase program to open the suitcase file—you do understand what I mean, don't you?" you'll understand when I say Steve Brecher should be canonized for creating Suitcase but crucified for naming it what he did. The latest version is called Suitcase 2 (not to be confused with Suitcase II). Aarrghh!

SuperFloppy Common name for Apple's *FDHD floppy disk drive,* which reads and writes 400K, 800K, and 1.44 *megabyte* disks.

supertwist An inexpensive type of liquid crystal display *(LCD),* with lower contrast and a narrower viewing angle than the costlier *active matrix* type. The *PowerBook* 100 and 140 use supertwist displays.

support 1) To offer a feature, as in, "This program supports rotated text and infinite zooming."

2) The most difficult job in the computer industry, bar none: helping your company's customers figure out how to actually use what your company's programmers and engineers have created and your company's salespeople have sold.

surge suppressor A device meant to smooth out the occasional voltage surges present in most electrical systems in order to prevent them from damaging your computer equipment. Where do these surges come from? Most people think first of lightning, but a much more common source is ordinary motor-driven devices like furnace blowers, refrigerators, and air conditioners. Every time an appliance that draws a substantial amount of current turns on or off, a voltage spike goes through your house wiring.

Modern computers have power supplies that protect them reasonably well against small spikes, but the occasional big one—or even too many small ones over a period of time— can do real damage to expensive equipment; hence the need for surge suppressors. By far the most common type of suppressor is one that uses inexpensive (25¢) devices called MOVs (metal oxide varistors) to shunt the surge energy onto the ground line, preventing it from reaching the computer. Unfortunately, there are three problems with this type of suppressor. First, MOVs wear out surprisingly fast. Each surge absorbed by an MOV decreases its effectiveness a bit, until in as little as six months it's no longer able to do its job. Second, when a really big surge hits, MOVs can arc over or even physically explode, presenting a serious fire hazard (especially if the unit has a plastic case). Third, dumping surge energy onto the ground line is like sweeping it under the rug—it doesn't really go away; it just pops up somewhere else. In this case, that may mean a few thousand volts suddenly appearing on the ground line of the cable running to your *modem* or *LAN* connection—which can mean big trouble!

Various alternative schemes have been tried in order to get around the problems with MOVs. The most effective I've seen is used in "surge eliminators" made by Zero Surge Inc., which use non-degrading components in a circuit that stores the surge energy, then slowly dribbles it back into the neutral line at a safe, controlled rate.

SYLK (SILK) SYmbolic LinK. A file format used for *spreadsheet* information. Since most spreadsheet programs can understand files saved in SYLK format, it serves as a medium of exchange between different programs.

SyQuest drive A *hard disk drive* whose disk is in a removable cartridge. These are widely used as *backup* devices, and to transport very large documents to *service bureaus* for printout. Most SyQuest drives hold 42.6 MB of data per cartridge, although newer models with twice the capacity are also available.

sysop (SIS OP) SYStem OPerator. A person who manages a computer bulletin board system *(BBS)*.

System Short for *operating system*. A program that lives in your *System Folder* and controls and coordinates all the different parts of the computer: hardware, software, what goes in, and what comes out. The System knows how to talk to the *disk drives*, *modem*, and *printer ports*, as well as how to display text and pictures on the Mac's screen. The System understands only special "computer-language" commands. You can't talk to it directly, so the *Finder* (or whatever program you're using) acts as your interpreter when dealing with the System. The System also contains *fonts, desk accessories*, and sounds, which can be viewed and moved around by double-clicking the System file to open it. It's important to have the correct version of the System, Finder, and related files for your particular Mac. You can get the latest versions from a dealer or from your local *user group*.

System

System Folder Sort of like a utility closet where the tools needed for various household chores are kept. These include the *System, Finder, printer driv-*

System Folder

ers, and a variety of other useful files your Mac needs to do its work. With System 7, many of the System Folder's contents are organized into subfolders: *Apple Menu Items, Control Panels, Extensions, Preferences, PrintMonitor Documents,* and *Startup Items* are among the most common.

System Heap A piece of *RAM* (memory) that the System reserves for its own use. An assortment of esoterica resides there, including various *patches*, device *drivers*, and *INITs (extensions)*. Under older versions of the Mac's system software (before System 7), the System Heap could become overcrowded with too many INITs, leading to crashes and other unruly behavior. Utilities like Bootman and Heap Fixer were created to let you expand the heap in order to reduce the chances of this happening. Under System 7, however, the System Heap is automatically and continuously resized. Thus, it never runs out of room, and these utilities are unnecessary.

System 7 Apple's latest major revision to the Mac *operating system*. System 7 introduced a host of improvements, including a *Finder* that actually finds things, *aliases, stationery* documents, *TrueType* fonts, *publish* and *subscribe, file sharing, balloon help, virtual memory,* and many other goodies. As always with major system software revisions, a lot of third-party software stopped working when System 7.0 came out, and a hasty round of revisions ensued. Most programs now work fine, but be wary of older *public domain* and *shareware* programs, whose authors may not have brought them up to date.

System 7 compatible Able to run under System 7 without *crashing* or malfunctioning.

System 7 savvy Able to take advantage of System 7 features like *balloon help* and *publish* and *subscribe.*

S

Tt

tab-delimited A data file saved from a *spreadsheet* or *database* program in a specific format: every item is separated from every other item by a tab character, and each row or group of items ends with a carriage return. In this form, the file can be read by many other programs.

Taligent A sure winner in the "Worst Company Name Based on a Pun" category, this organization with the uninTaligent-sounding moniker is the fruit of the Apple-IBM Mutual Nonaggression Pact. In a manner somewhat reminiscent of Hitler and Stalin back in 1939, the two erst-  while enemies have agreed to join forces against a common foe that threatens their plans for world domination— in this case, *Microsoft,* which has some pretty ambitious plans of its own. Their alliance has resulted in Taligent, a company formed to develop Apple's advanced *Pink* system software running on IBM's advanced POWERPC RS/6000 *microprocessor.* Supposedly, the resulting system will be licensed to all comers, thus ushering in a veritable golden age wherein all software will run, trouble-free, on all computers, and the lion shall lie down with the lamb. Uh huh. Sure. Hitler invaded Russia in 1941, less than two years after signing his pact with Stalin. Any bets on how long this alliance will last?

Tall Adjusted An option in the *ImageWriter* Page Setup dialog, it makes certain that text and graphics are printed in the same height-to-width proportions as they appear on screen. (The compensation is necessary because the ImageWriter normally prints about 10 percent more dots per inch horizontally than vertically, resulting in tall, rectangular pixels.) If you're using an ImageWriter and you want your circles to be circular, your squares to be square, and your text not to be squashed horizontally, always turn on Tall Adjusted before printing! (Don't ask me why Apple didn't make this the *default* mode.)

TCP/IP Transmission Control Protocol/Internet Protocol. A standard that lets you move data files and *electronic mail* between *networked* computers that normally speak different languages. Examples: *IBM* mainframes, *Sun workstations* and, yes, even Macs.

TeachText The simplest of Mac word processors, TeachText was devised so that users would always have an easy way to open the ubiquitous *"Read Me"* files that come with new software. Originally, TeachText simply read plain *ASCII* text files, but its latest versions can also view *PICT* images and play *QuickTime* movies.

TeachText

tear-off menu A menu (for example, the Tools menu in *HyperCard*) that can be "torn off" the menubar and used as a free-floating *palette*. To tear off the menu, you pull it down and then keep pulling past the end of the menu, or pull sideways.

tech support See *support*.

telecommunications Using a computer to talk to another computer, usually over the phone. To do this, you need a *modem*, which converts your computer's data to an audible form that can be sent through the phone lines, and a *terminal emulator* program, which helps you communicate with the other computer.

template A guide; in computer jargon, a fill-in-the-blanks document that you can use as the framework for a finished piece of work. For example, a newsletter template might be a PageMaker document with the publication's logo already in place and with preset columns, rules, type styles, and other elements—everything but the words and pictures. All you have to do is pour your stories into the columns, place your illustrations, and voilà: a newsletter!

10BaseT A type of wiring often used for *Ethernet* networks. Why the weird name? Well, it stands for 10 megabits per second (the data transmission rate) baseband (just data, no carrier—and don't worry if you don't know what that means!) and *twisted pair* wire (as opposed to coaxial cable). It's a medium-performance, relatively inexpensive wiring system that's rapidly becoming the most popular way to do Ethernet.

terminal emulator   A program that lets your computer talk to another computer (such as a private *BBS*) or network (like *AOL*) over the phone using a *modem*. This is a relatively modern convenience. In the early days, computers were large, room-filling clusters of equipment, and users communicated with them using terminals, which were basically keyboards with a video display but no "brains." When self-contained personal computers became available, people who wanted to communicate with large computers wrote programs to make their personal computers emulate, or imitate, the old dumb terminals. Today's programs (such as ZTerm and MicroPhone) do much more than emulate terminals—they have file-transfer capabilities and built-in programming languages that let them perform many tasks automatically.

termination   Not as ominous as it sounds, this is something you have to watch out for with *SCSI* equipment like hard disks and scanners. It's a way of preventing signals from bouncing around and causing confusion. Imagine that you're standing at one end of a long, tile-lined hallway, shouting to someone at the other end. Your voice echoes up and down the hall, making it difficult for your friend to understand what you're saying. But if you put big pieces of cotton batting at either end of the hallway, they would soak up some of the echoes and keep them from bouncing back and forth so much. This is how termination works: you put a group of resistors at each end of an electrical circuit (like a SCSI *bus*) to soak up the signal echoes that would otherwise bounce back and forth. The rules say "one set of terminators at each end of the SCSI chain"; in practice, that's only a starting place in what can be a lengthy trial-and-error process. You may end up with one set of terminators—or three!

T

With SCSI termination, the gurus will tell you, "If it works, it works...and don't ask why."

text file A file containing only *ASCII* (American Standard Code for Information Interchange) text. Most *word processors* save their documents in special formats, which contain not only the actual words of the document but also information about words in boldface or *italic*, different *fonts* and sizes, embedded illustrations, and so forth. An ASCII text file, on the other hand, contains just the words you typed, plus a few formatting characters like carriage returns and tabs. It's the lowest common denominator of files, understandable by all word processors, so it's often used for documentation purposes, where the program's publisher doesn't know which word processor a user may have. *TeachText* can open any text file.

thermal printer A printer that uses heat to create an image. Thermal printers use special paper (the same kind used in common *fax* machines), which darkens when heated. An array of tiny heating elements—one for each printed dot—presses against the paper and creates a dot-matrix image of letters, numbers and graphics on the paper. Thermal printers are very quiet and compact, so they work well with portable computers (Kodak's battery-powered Diconix printers are a good example). On the other hand, their resolution is mediocre, and that waxy-feeling, fast-fading thermal paper is a definite drawback. Technically, *thermal wax printers* are also thermal printers, but they're different enough to rate their own definition.

thermal transfer A printer mechanism that works by heating a wax-coated ribbon in order to transfer tiny dots of hot colored wax to paper. Low-priced color printers are mostly based on this technology. It's slow (up to five minutes per page) and the quality is mediocre at best, but it's an affordable way to get color output.

thermal wax printer A printer that uses heated wax to form an image. The wax is in the form of a thin coating on an "image roll" that's pressed into contact with a sheet of paper. In turn, an array of tiny heating elements presses against the image roll. When a heating element is pulsed, it melts a tiny area of the waxed image roll and transfers a droplet of colored wax to the paper. Thermal wax technology is mostly used in medium-priced color printers.

third-party Not made by Apple, as in, "You can save a lot of money by buying a third-party hard disk drive instead of one of Apple's."

32-bit addressing Heeding the incessant cry of "I need more RAM!" from power-hungry users, Apple has given us the means to address up to four *gigabytes* of memory—
4,294,967,296 bytes, to be exact—with System 7. (That's just over $122,000 worth of RAM at today's prices...a mere pittance!) It's done by using a 32-bit-wide address—hence the name. Unfortunately, there are complications. First, many Macs have hardware that can't take advantage of 32-bit addressing. None of the 68000-based machines like the *Mac Plus*, the original SE and Classic, the Mac Portable, and the *PowerBook* 100 can do this. Second, many of the older Macs—the SE/30, II, IIx, and IIcx—had a bug in their *ROMs* that prevented using 32-bit addressing. Third, a lot of the software now in use crashes messily when you try to run it in 32-bit mode because its programmers failed to follow Apple's *rules*.

There's no fix for the 68000-based machines, short of a processor-replacing upgrade from a company like Dove or Daystar. For the machines with buggy ROMs, there's *MODE32*, a free fix distributed by Apple in the form of an *extension*. You just drop it into your System Folder and it cures the problem. As far as the incompatible software is concerned, responsible companies are cleaning up their code as fast as they can and putting out updated, "32-bit clean" versions. Eventually this problem will fade away, but right now it pays to ask before you buy.

32-bit clean Software that's able to run on a Mac using *32-bit addressing* without nasty crashes and other side effects.

thumb   One name for the small white box in a *scroll bar*. Dragging the thumb up and down is a quick way to scroll a window. Why is it called a thumb? Because its creators thought of it as being like a sliding control that you'd move with your thumb. In fact, if you have System 7 and a color or grayscale display, you'll notice that the box now has little ridges—presumably to keep your thumb from slipping off!

TIFF   (TIFF)   Tagged Image File Format. A type of *bitmapped* image file (usually created by a *scanner*). TIFF files can include color or *grayscale* information (up to 24-bit color), or they may be strictly black and white. Unfortunately, there are many variants of this format, and not all applications understand all TIFF files. To make things more complicated, TIFF files from DOS computers are not compatible with Mac TIFF format because they're stored in Intel's wacky byte-swapped format, where every other byte is exchanged with its neighbor. (Like this: "every where byte other exchanged is its with neighbor." Don't ask why they do this. It's *DOS*. What can I tell ya?) Despite all this, TIFF is the closest thing to a universal format for bitmapped images.

title bar   The top part of a Macintosh window; it contains the window's title (not surprisingly), the *close box*, and (in most cases) the *zoom box*. Clicking anywhere in a window makes it active (which means that you can work on its contents); an active window shows horizontal lines in its title bar. If you want to move a window, you can click in its title bar and drag it.

toggle   To alternate between two states, like a lamp switch that turns on when you push it, then off when you push it again. For example, if you click on a *check box* that says "Show invisibles," the box becomes checked and the option is turned on; clicking again turns off the option and unchecks the box. The button is said to toggle between its two possible conditions.

Token Ring   An IBM standard for computer networks, this gets its name from the scheme it uses to avoid "collisions"—the result of everybody trying to talk at once. For example, in an AppleTalk network, if two computers happen to start sending at exactly the same instant, both will immediately sense the collision, stop, wait for a short, random interval, and try again. Because the delay is random for each machine, chances are that no collision will occur the second time around.

But this "back off and wait" strategy wastes precious time and slows down the network. So IBM came up with another method: arrange the network like a ring and have the computers take turns sending. How do they know whose turn it is? They pass around a "token," a packet of data that gives the computer holding it permission to send whatever data it wants to without fear of collision. If it has nothing to say, it simply passes the token to the next computer, giving that one permission to talk. And it always passes the token after a fixed time no matter what—that way no one machine can hold onto the token indefinitely and monopolize the network! This orderly, efficient strategy eliminates wasted time due to collisions. Although Macs normally use other collision-avoidance methods, they can connect to Token Ring networks using Apple's TokenTalk software.

TokenTalk Apple's software that lets Macs connect to networks using the *Token Ring protocol.*

toner The black powder inside a *LaserWriter* cartridge that's used to form an image on paper. It consists of very finely ground carbon and styrene plastic. Attracted to the printer's light-sensitive drum where the laser beam has struck, it's transferred to a sheet of paper and then *fused* permanently by heat and pressure.

Toolbox A collection of program modules that do basic things like displaying windows, menus, and so on. Part of your Mac's *operating system,* the Toolbox resides partly in permanent *ROM* memory and partly in the *System* file, which is loaded piecemeal from disk when needed. By making "calls" to the Toolbox, Macintosh programs can have these basic chores performed for them in standard ways, saving programmers the trouble of recreating commonly used pieces of pro-gram *code* and helping to ensure a standard look and feel for all Mac programs—no triangular windows or sideways menubars!

topology In computer usage, the shape or form of a computer *network*. Common network topologies are the *daisychain*, backbone, ring, and star—the names are pretty much self-descriptive.

TOPS (TOPS) An old, buggy commercial networking prod-uct. Incompatible with Apple's *AFP* networking standard, TOPS was once fairly common but has now been replaced by other methods such as *AppleShare* and System 7's *file sharing*.

track A circular area on a hard disk or floppy disk, analo-gous to a track on a record or CD. When your Mac needs to read a file from the disk, it tells the disk drive to move its *read/write heads* to the track where the file begins.

trackball A *cursor*-positioning device similar in principle to an upside-down mouse: to move the cursor, you roll a ball with your finger. Takes up less desk space than a mouse, but is not very useful for freehand graphics. People seem to either love or hate them, so try it out before you buy one.

tracking Changing the spacing between all the letters in a select- **tightly tracked text** ed piece of text. This differs from *kerning*, which refers to changing the space between two individual letters.

transparent Said of software that's "invisible" to the user, or at least requires no extra thought on the user's part. For example, once Adobe Type Manager is installed, its operation is transparent to the user—type simply looks better on screen, but you don't have to do anything differently than you did before. The old advertising slogan "Set it and forget it" captures the idea of transparency pretty well.

trapping In current usage (mis-usage, some would say), this means to ensure that adjacent but differently colored graphics or text overlap slightly. This pre-

trap   no trap

vents white gaps from showing up when the printing plates for the various colors fail to line up perfectly on the press. Traditionally, this tricky process is called using chokes and spreads (it depends on which graphic is overlapped onto what).

Trash The little image of a trash can that sits at the lower right of your Mac's *desktop*. It's used for deleting files and folders and (confusingly) for ejecting—not erasing!—floppies. (There are historical reasons for the "drag the floppy to the Trash" shortcut, but frankly it's never made sense to me or to anyone else I know.) With System 7, items stay in the Trash until you manually empty it—but if you're still using an earlier System (like 6.0.7), the Trash is emptied automatically whenever you copy files, run a program, or shut down, so don't count on those discarded files staying around.

Trinitron A high-quality color picture tube (*CRT*) of a special design, made by Sony. Unlike conventional tubes with their tiny phosphor dots, Trinitron tubes have vertical phosphor stripes. More important, Sony substitutes a tightly stretched wire grid for the distortion-prone internal shadow mask used in other color tubes; the result is a sharper, brighter picture than most competitors. Apple's 13" color *monitor* uses a Trinitron tube, as do most of the better color video monitors on the market. One side effect of the Trinitron's wire grid is a very faint gray horizontal line visible about a quarter of the way up from the bottom on most Trinitrons. It's caused by a tensioning wire that helps stabilize the grid.

Trojan horse A seemingly harmless program that acts as a carrier for a computer *virus*. A recent example was the game program "Obnoxious Tetris," which carried and spread the so-called "Michelangelo" virus—a time bomb designed to erase the hard disks of *DOS* computers on March 6 of each year. Public-domain games, which are quickly copied and passed around among users, are the most likely to be used as Trojan horses. To protect yourself against this type of maliciousness, make sure your Mac is protected by an anti-virus program such as *Disinfectant*.

TrueImage An imitation *PostScript* interpreter originally created by Bauer and later purchased by Microsoft. Licensed to printer makers like Abaton, it's one of the less *buggy* PostScript *clones*. Just the same, as the song says, "Ain't nothin' like the real thing, baby!"

TrueType Apple's name for the *outline font* technology built into System 7. TrueType provides some of the same benefits as *Adobe Type Manager:* it gives you better-looking text on the screen and lets inexpensive high-resolution printers like Hewlett-Packard's DeskWriter produce high-quality output at any type size desired. However, TrueType uses its own *proprietary* font format and is incompatible with industry-standard *PostScript* fonts. Also, it works with text only—unlike PostScript, which is a full-featured graphical language for text and all kinds of images.

turbo Meaningless, sales-oriented buzzword, designed to give an impression of speed. You can roughly translate it as, "We think you're dumb enough to buy this"...as in Turbo Pascal ("We think you're dumb enough to buy this Pascal"), Turbo Laser printer, Turbo Trackball, and so on.

Turing test A common-sense test of computer intelligence proposed by the British mathematician Alan Turing. As you can imagine, there's always been a lot of argument about what would constitute a truly intelligent computer. Turing suggested this test: put a person in a room with a computer terminal, connect it to a computer in another room, and let the person converse with the computer. If after a reasonable length of time the person is unable to say whether there's a computer or a human on the other end of the line, then for practical purposes that computer can be considered to have human-level intelligence. So far, no machine has passed the Turing test, but it seems to be only a matter of time.

tweak To make a minor adjustment or improvement, as in, "The program's almost ready, but the *code* needs a little tweaking." (Translation: "With luck, we hope to get it working by next summer.")

tween A contraction of "inbetween," which is animator's slang for the job of creating frames in between the "key frames" that define significant poses in an action sequence. Here's how it was traditionally done. Suppose you wanted to show an ice cube melting. The animator would draw two or three key frames: a frozen ice cube, a half-melted cube, a puddle of water. Then an "inbetweener" (an apprentice animator) would draw the in-between frames that showed the melting cube in its intermediate stages, while the animator went on to draw key frames for the next sequence. This production-line animation system was used for over fifty years by Disney and the other major studios. Nowadays, computers can do much of the tweening, relieving humans of yet another tedious chore.

twisted pair A cable consisting of a pair of wires, twisted together to reduce interference pickup (straight parallel wires act as an antenna, picking up—and radiating—unwanted signals). Your telephone wiring is an example, though it has two pairs in a single cable. With the right kind of wire *(10BaseT)*, twisted pair can be used to build *Ethernet* networks less expensively than with the older *coaxial* cable method.

Type 1 font A *PostScript* font that's compressed, so it takes up less room, and *hinted*, so it prints better at small sizes on low-resolution devices. Type 1 fonts are by far the most common outline fonts now in use; at last count there were well over 6,000 different Type 1 typefaces available. They're also the only ones that will work with Adobe Type Manager *(ATM)*.

Type 2 font There ain't no such thing! This standard was proposed but never implemented.

Type 3 font A format for *PostScript* fonts no longer in use, having been largely superseded by *Type 1*. Type 3 fonts are larger in file size and don't print as well on low-resolution printers like the 300-*dpi LaserWriters*, and they don't work with Adobe Type Manager *(ATM)*.

typesetting The act of placing letters on a page. In common usage, this means creating the high-quality text for a *camera-ready copy* of a document. Once done by hot-lead machines like the Linotype and Monotype, then by phototypesetters, this task has now been taken over by computer-driven *imagesetters*, which work from PostScript files to create not only type but graphics as well.

Uu

Unix A large, complex *operating system* designed in the sixties at Bell Labs. Originally designed for *mainframes* and *mini*computers, Unix is now also used on some desktop computers, including Macs. (A/UX is Apple's version of Unix for the Mac, but fewer than 1% of Mac owners use it.) Unix was designed as a *multitasking* operating system in the days when computers were expensive devices that were shared between many users. The benefits of placing this kind of system on a single-user personal computer are unclear, and the drawbacks—an enormous appetite for memory, processor power and disk space—are significant. Many incompatible versions of Unix exist, and proponents can often be found arguing with near-religious fervor about the vices and virtues of their favorites.

update 1) An improved version of a program, offering enhanced features, bug fixes, or changes to make it compatible with newer versions of the Mac's *operating system*. Users are generally charged for software updates; in fact, they're an important source of revenue for companies like Microsoft, whose periodic upgrades to programs like Word and Excel can cost well over a hundred dollars. If you own a number of programs, updates can easily cost you several hundred dollars a year—so be sure to figure them into your budget.

2) The process of redrawing the image on your Mac's screen after something has been moved or changed (see *refresh rate*).

upload The opposite of *download;* to send a document (for example, an *electronic mail* message or a file) to another computer or computer *network* (for example, AOL, *CompuServe,* or a *BBS).* You do this by using a *modem* to communicate with the other computer over the phone.

U

UPS Uninterruptible Power Supply. A box that can take over and keep your Mac running when the power fails. It contains batteries, a charger, and an inverter circuit that turns the DC from the batteries into 120V AC for your Mac. When power fails, a sensor switches the UPS over to battery power, giving you time to complete your job and shut down. If your business (or your network!) depends on your Mac being available, you should have a UPS.

user group Your fellow sufferers. They're the best source of help when things go wrong, because they've been through it all before. I've solved far more Mac problems with advice from user group members than I have by asking local dealers for help! User groups typically offer training, expert advice, informative newsletters, and libraries of *public-domain* and *shareware* programs—all for two or three dollars a month, less than the cover price of most magazines. For the user group nearest you, call Apple's user group hotline at 800-538-9696, ext. 500.

user interface The way the computer looks to you, the user; the way you interact with it. Early personal computers like the IBM PC gave you a blank screen with a "prompt" like A>; you were expected to remember a catalog of cryptic commands and type in the one you wanted in order to tell the computer what to do. The Mac was the first computer to popularize the "graphical user interface" concept, in which you do things like copying and deleting files by dragging icons around the screen and clicking on screen "buttons." As you probably know, this friendlier, more visually oriented approach is now being copied by every other computer maker, including IBM.

utility An *application* that performs some useful "housekeeping" task, such as backing up your files or installing fonts. Examples include DiskFit Pro (backup), the Norton Utilities (disk repair and file recovery), and *Disinfectant* (virus protection).

Vv

vaporware There's *hardware*—stuff that's real, substantial, and will likely break your foot if you drop it. Then there's *software*—just a bunch of bytes on a disk, but it has real, substantial features (and a price tag to match). And then there's vaporware: software that was announced, oh, maybe eight or ten months ago and still isn't shipping. Perhaps the most famous case was the late, unlamented FullWrite Professional, which arrived eighteen months late after a series of excuses that have never been topped ("We were all ready to ship, but the truck with the manuals was hijacked on its way to the plant"). When you hear the phrase "Real soon now..." *(RSN)* you can be sure there's vaporware lurking nearby.

VAR (VAR) Value-Added Reseller. A company that buys equipment, incorporates it into a larger system, then sells it to users (generally at a substantial profit). For example, if you're in the graphic arts business and decide that it's time to computerize, you may not want to spend the time to figure out what hardware and software to buy and how to hook it all together; but you could go to a VAR who will sell you a system comprising a *Mac IIfx*, *LaserWriter*, *scanner*, and software, all set up and ready to go. VARs usually arrange for training, too, as part of their service.

vector graphics Another term for *object-oriented* graphics (a vector is a line segment, a type of graphical object). These images are created from geometric objects like lines and circles, as opposed to *bitmapped* graphics.

verify To double-check a file that has just been copied to a disk, in order to make sure it's the same as the original. The *Finder* copies a file in three steps: First, it reads the original file into *RAM* (memory). Then it writes the file from memory to the disk. Finally, it reads back the disk file that was just written and compares it with the version still in memory, in order to verify that the new file is identical to the original.

version Computer programs are always being improved (and *debugged*!) by their creators, and it's often important to know whether you have the latest version of a program. When you're running a program, the top item on your *Apple menu* usually says something like "About this program." Choosing the "About..." item brings up a message box telling you what version you have, who wrote it, and other useful information. (Another way to find the version of a program is to use the Finder's *Get Info* command.) Caution: if you ever run into a program with a version number like 2.0b5, beware! That "b" means this is a *beta* or prerelease version of the program and is almost certain to contain bugs!

video board A plug-in circuit board (usually a *NuBus* board) that produces a video signal that can be displayed on a video *monitor*. Video boards come in many versions, from those designed to work with two-page monochrome monitors to those offering 24 or even 32 bits of *color* on a variety of screen sizes.

videodisc A plastic disc, 8" or 12" in diameter, that looks like a big version of a compact digital audio disc (CD) and has up to two hours of very high quality video (movies or other information) recorded on it. Although the video is not in digital form, the audio portion is often encoded digitally just like a CD. These discs offer much the same advantages as CDs: far higher picture and sound quality than tape; long life, due to the fact that they're played by a laser beam instead of being rubbed against a tape head; and extremely quick (less than one second) access to any part of the program. Also like CDs, they can't be recorded on with home equipment. Beloved by movie collectors for their unequalled quality and durability, videodiscs are also of special interest to designers of educational and *multimedia* systems, because a disc player can be controlled by a Mac, making possible some very interesting *interactive* software.

video RAM Memory used to store the pictures that are displayed on a computer's screen. Often called *VRAM*.

Video Toaster A video processor (actually an Amiga 500 computer in a box) that you can connect to the Mac. It lets you *overlay* computer graphics on live video, and do various special effects—warps, fades, and the like—then output broadcast-quality *NTSC* video—the kind you can record on a VCR. The Toaster is an inexpensive way to do high quality video, but it suffers from its un-Mac-like, Amiga-based software. For example, it can overlay text on video very nicely—but only using *proprietary* fonts (available solely from the Toaster's manufacturer, NewTek). No *PostScript*. No *TrueType*. No choice. But if you can live with a somewhat klutzy interface and a meager choice of typefaces, it's the biggest bargain around.

Views A control panel that lets you customize some of the ways the *Finder* displays your files and folders. For example,

```
┌─ Icon Views ───────────────────────┐
│                                     │
│   ▯ ▯ ▯ ▯   ◉ Straight grid         │
│                                     │
│   ▯ ▯ ▯ ▯   ○ Staggered grid        │
│                                     │
└─────────────────────────────────────┘
```

you can choose to have your icons snap to an invisible grid (great for neatniks like me!), either in straight or staggered rows. Having trouble reading those tiny filenames in 9 point Geneva? Use Views to change them to 18 point Helvetica, and make it easy on your eyes. That's one nice thing about the Mac—you can change it to suit your own style.

virtual Translates roughly as "imitation"—as in *virtual reality* or *virtual memory*.

virtual memory (VM) A scheme for making your Macintosh think that the empty space on your hard disk drive is really *RAM* (memory). Since the cost

Virtual Memory

○ On
◉ Off

per megabyte of hard disk storage is much lower than the cost per meg of RAM, this is a way to save money if you need to run large, memory-hungry programs. It has two disadvantages: First, you can't do it unless your Mac has the needed hardware, namely either a 68030 (or later) *microprocessor* or a 68851 *PMMU* (Paged Memory

Management Unit) chip. Second, because hard disk storage is far slower than RAM, you'll pay a penalty in speed.

virtual reality (VR) A realistic simulated environment (created by a computer) complete with three-dimensional images and stereo sound. You can enter the scene and interact with it: an image of your hand follows its movements as you pick up simulated objects, examine them, even play catch with other participants! How is all this done? Well, in a "classic" *VR* setup, you wear stereoscopic video goggles and stereo headphones. Not only do you see a 3D environment—if you turn your head, the scene shifts naturally before your eyes, creating a startlingly real illusion. Stereo sounds are likewise panned right or left as you move your head. For input, you wear "DataGloves," which tell the computer what your hands are doing so that a computer-generated image of a hand can replicate their actions before your eyes.

There are many other kinds of VR. For example, imagine a large-screen projected computer image of a tree hung with pots and pans. As you stand in front of the image, a video camera connected to the same computer takes your own likeness and literally puts you in the scene. When you move your hands to "touch" the pots and pans, they ring with the notes of the musical scale! Pretty soon you're playing tunes on your virtual xylophone.

Virtual reality has one key requirement: lots and lots of computer power. Although present-day Macs can do some limited VR, it'll be a while before we see really sophisticated virtual environments running in the Mac. Meanwhile, we can try to figure out what to do with it when we get it!

virus A program fragment that can attach itself to other programs (including your *System* and *Finder)* and spread from machine to machine. Like a biological virus, it's power- less by itself but can infect another program and use it to make copies of the virus. (For related examples of malignant code, see *Trojan horse* and *worm.)* Depending on the maliciousness of its creator, it may cause programs to randomly *bomb*, erase disk files, or worse. The most common viruses on the Mac are *nVIR* and *WDEF*. To prevent your Mac from becoming infected, use the free *Disinfectant* program (available from your local *user group*) to check all new programs and disks for infection before running them. And always keep your master (original) program disks locked!

VLF Very Low Frequency. Electromagnetic radiation emitted by appliances such as computer video monitors. There's a possibility it may have adverse effects on humans (see *ELF*).

VLSI Very Large Scale Integration. A term applied to an integrated circuit *chip* with more than 10,000 transistors. Considering that all those transistors must fit on a sliver of silicon the size of your little fingernail, perhaps "Very Small Scale Integration" would have been more appropriate. Just for comparison, the original 1984 Mac's 68000 *microprocessor* had—surprise!—68,000 transistors (give or take a dozen). But that's nothing nowadays; more recent chips like the 68040 have close to a million!

VM See *virtual memory*.

volume A *hard disk, floppy disk*, or a disk *partition*. I could go into technical details, but here's a working definition: if it appears in the upper right area of your *desktop* and you can store files in it, it's a volume.

VR See *virtual reality*.

VRAM (VEE ram) See *video RAM*.

V.32 (VEE dot thirty two) An international standard for sending files via *modem*. A V.32 modem can send data at speeds up to 9600 bits per second. It automatically checks to make sure the file gets through error-free and resends any parts that are garbled in transit.

V.32bis (VEE dot thirty two biss) An international standard for sending files via *modem*. Similar to *v.32*, but a V.32bis modem can send data at speeds up to 14,400 bits per second. It automatically checks to make sure the file gets through error-free and resends any parts that are garbled in transit.

V.42 (VEE DOT FORTY TWO)   An international standard for error correction when sending files via *modem*. V.42 is similar to *MNP 4*, but its error correction performs better. If data gets scrambled by a bad phone connection, a V.42 modem retransmits as necessary to make sure the info gets through perfectly.

V.42bis (VEE DOT FORTY TWO BISS)   An international standard for data compression when sending files via *modem*. V.42bis is similar to *MNP 5*, but its compression is more efficient; this means that files get there faster. In addition, V.42bis modems compress data only when it's advantageous to do so. Files that are already compressed (with *StuffIt* or similar utilities) are left alone. This contrasts with MNP 5, which tries to put the squeeze on everything it sends—and can actually slow down when transmitting already-compressed files. V.42bis requires that *V.42* error correction also be present.

Ww

Wacom tablet A superb *graphics tablet* (an input device that lets you use a pen-like stylus instead of a mouse). It has a cordless, batteryless, pressure-sensitive stylus that can work with software like Photoshop or Painter to create the illusion of a paintbrush, a marker pen, a charcoal stick—anything you want. If you're an artist, take my word for it: this is the only graphics tablet worth considering. Don't even think about anything else.

WAN (wan) Wide Area Network. A *network* of computers spread over a fairly large geographical area—as opposed to a local area network *(LAN)*, which usually links up machines in one building. A WAN uses microwave links, high-speed digital phone lines (see *ISDN*), or even satellite communications to tie together a company's regional offices into one big network.

WDEF (W deff) A common and highly infectious *virus* that infects the *desktop* file on a disk (hard or floppy). When an infected disk is inserted into a "clean" Mac, it immediately infects the desktops of any other disks present. Because it contains programming errors, WDEF can cause crashes, disk damage, and other odd behavior. WDEF comes in several strains; all can be detected and removed by antivirus programs like *Disinfectant*.

widow A displeasingly short line of type, as when the first line of a paragraph ends up all by itself at the bottom of a page, or the last line appears at the top of the following page. Although there are heated arguments about the difference between a widow and an *orphan*, for practical purposes they can be considered synonymous—and equally to be avoided!

wildcard 1) A character such as "?" that can be used as a match for any other character in a search operation. For example, many programs let you use "Peters?n" as a search string to find all occurrences of both "Peterson" and "Petersen." Some programs also let you use a separate wildcard character (such as "*") as a stand-in for any number of unknown letters, letting you use "Kre*z" to find both "Kreuz" and "Kreutz."

2) *HyperCard's* original name while it was in development. The name was changed to avoid a trademark conflict, but if you look at the *creator* of a HyperCard *stack,* you'll see that it's "WILD"—a legacy of the product's almost-forgotten past. Personally, I wish they had left it the way it was— "WildTalk" scripting language and all!

windoid A special kind of Macintosh window; often used for tool *palettes* in programs like *HyperCard* and *Illustrator.* Windoids "float" in front of all other windows, so they're always available and never get buried under  other windows. (Only an *alert* or *dialog box* can be in front of a windoid.) A windoid is easy to recognize because of the distinctive patterned "drag bar" at its top (where a normal window would have its *title bar).*

window A rectangular area of your screen that can be used to look at a document (like a text file) or a collection of icons (like a folder). The document can be much larger than the window, just as your back yard is much larger than your kitchen window, but you can still see the whole document through the window by viewing one part at a time (that's what *scroll bars* are for). Almost all Macintosh windows have standard features such as a *title bar, close box,* and *zoom box.*

A little-known fact is that it's possible to create round windows and other bizarre shapes and graft them onto standard programs. The exact methods are a closely guarded secret known only to the inner circle of the Mac-adept; if you ever turn

on your Mac and find that your Finder windows have all become circular, you'll know your machine has been touched by one of the chosen few.

Windows Microsoft's attempt to convince *DOS* users that their machines can be "just as good" as a Mac. Even though most DOS users aren't buying this fantasy, many say that while Windows may not be as sophisticated as the Mac's OS, it's "good enough." In any case, since few computer owners are willing to admit that the hardware and software they've spent so much time and money on are obsolete, millions of *PC* owners have bought Windows in hopes of making their PCs look more up-to-date. However, there are some fundamental problems.

Unlike the Mac's *operating system,* which was designed as a graphical *user interface* from the ground up, Windows is actually just a thin layer of imitation-Mac windows and icons plastered over the *command line*-based, user-hostile DOS operating system. Because every command has to be passed down from layer to layer before finally being executed, Windows is large and inefficient. A much bigger problem, though, is that Microsoft has done nothing to ensure that other software producers employ a consistent user interface in their programs for Windows. The result is that various Windows programs use widely differing methods to do the same jobs—unlike Mac programs, which all use the same menus and commands for functions like opening, saving, and printing files. Windows' jumble of inconsistent interfaces means that each program has to be learned separately—a tremendous drawback for users.

Despite all this, millions of copies of Windows have been sold, and many popular Mac programs like PageMaker have been *ported* to the Windows environment. Although its basic structure makes Windows more than a little bit of a *kluge,* its users don't seem to care, and the system appears destined to become a standard. Even Apple is bringing some of its more innovative concepts to Windows in hope of establishing *QuickTime* and *OCE* as industry-wide standards.

word processor A program that replaces a typewriter—and lets you do a whole lot more. A typewriter lets you create neat-looking printed documents. A word processor also lets you rearrange the text in your document, automatically check its spelling, incorporate pictures into it, change its typeface, and do many other useful things. A good word processor can't make you a better writer than you are, but it will let you be the best writer you're capable of being. If you want to get the most out of your word processor, read "The Mac is not a typewriter" by Robin Williams.

word wrap A function that moves a word from the end of one line of text to the beginning of the next line in order to prevent breaking or hyphenating it. Word wrap works automatically as you type, so you don't have to hit the return key at the end of every line as you would with a typewriter. In fact, hitting the return key is something you should do only at the end of a paragraph. Putting a return at the end of each line makes it impossible for word wrap to do its job, and is guaranteed to make editors tear their hair and foam at the mouth!

workstation A computer that can fit on a desktop but is more powerful than a "personal computer." Since a workstation is also a one-person computer, the distinction is fairly arbitrary. Some call a *Mac Quadra* a workstation; others say it's not powerful enough. Perhaps a good working definition is, "At any given time, a workstation is the most powerful single-person computer available." Computers made by Sun and Apollo are generally said to be typical workstations.

worm A program (usually malicious) designed to replicate itself and spread from one computer to another over a *network*. Unlike a *virus*, which must infect another program before it can do its work, a worm is self-sufficient. For example, in 1988 a worm was released on the Arpanet network. Spreading by exploiting a loophole in the *Unix electronic mail* facility, it disabled over 2,000 computers across the country in less than fifteen hours.

Large networks like the Arpanet and *Internet* are very vulnerable to worms; indeed, rumor has it that military planners are exploring their possible use as weapons of war.

WORM drive Write Once/Read Many. A data storage device based on optical techniques (similar to those used in CD-ROMs) that can be written only once but read back as often as desired—sort of like a pad of paper and an indelible pen. Its advantages are that it provides very large storage (often billions of bytes) at reasonable cost. The fact that it can't be erased is a limitation, but WORMs are suitable for archival purposes, where data need not be changed once stored. WORMs can be seen as a transitional stage, to be replaced in a few years by fully erasable optical storage devices.

Wozniak, Steve ("Woz") Co-inventor (with Steve *Jobs*) of the pioneering *Apple II* personal computer, and thus one of Apple's founding fathers. "Woz" and Jobs were *hackers* who at one point augmented their incomes by selling illegal "blue boxes" to their friends. (A blue box contained an electronic circuit that could generate specially coded tones; these would fool the phone company's switching centers into letting you make long-distance calls for free.) They both worked as engineers for Hewlett-Packard, but played with digital electronics in their spare time. When Woz built a simple, elegant single-board microcomputer, Jobs—a tireless promoter—persuaded him that they could make money selling the boards to other members of the Homebrew Computer Club...and the Apple was born.

Working out of a garage, with startup funds provided by the sale of Jobs' VW bus and Woz's *H-P* calculator (in the days when a calculator was a multi-hundred-dollar item!), they built and sold Apple I kits and later, fully-assembled Apple II computers. Conceived as a ready-to-run "appliance" computer, the Apple II had a sleek, modern-looking case and a built-in *BASIC* interpreter—both innovations at the time. With financial backing from venture capitalist Mike Markkula, Woz and Jobs turned the Apple II into a fabulously successful product: within five years the company had sold a billion dollars' worth of computers.

W

But things went sour with the Apple ///, Woz's attempt to break into the business market. Bad engineering, production screwups, and confused marketing added up to a colossal failure, and Apple was still licking its wounds when IBM unleashed the IBM PC. Neither cheap nor innovative, the PC was nonetheless an IBM standard, and it soon took the burgeoning business market right out of Apple's hands. Woz tinkered with a few more projects, then left Apple to promote a series of rock concerts that lost large amounts of money. At last report he was living in a huge, elaborate, underground home, equipped with state-of-the-art video games, an underground pool, and perhaps the world's largest collection of movies on *videodisc*.

wrap   Abbreviation for *word wrap;* to move a word from the end of one line of text to the beginning of the next line in order to prevent breaking or hyphenating it. Word wrap works automatically as you type, so you don't have to hit the return key at the end of every line as you would with a typewriter.

wristwatch   The shape the Mac's *pointer* changes to when the machine is busy doing something and can't respond to you for the time being. HyperCard uses a spinning "beach ball" shape for the same purpose.

write protect   To protect a file or disk from being changed, written to, or erased; to lock. For floppy disks, you do this by sliding the write-protect tab to the open (see-through) position. For documents or other files, you select the file, use the Finder's *Get Info* command, and click the box that says "Lock."

WYSIWYG   (WIZ ZEE WIG)   What You See Is What You Get. An ideal toward which the Macintosh strives. It means that what you see on the screen should correspond as closely as possible to what you get on paper when you print. This is one of the main philosophical differences between the Macintosh way of doing things and the *MS-DOS* way, in which the screen display bears little relationship to paper output.

Xx

XCMD (EX COMMAND) An "external" command added to *HyperCard* or to a HyperCard *stack*. One of HyperCard's greatest virtues is its ability to be extended beyond the built-in capabilities of the *HyperTalk* language. Suppose you want to eject a disk under program control, but you find there's no HyperTalk command to do this. Luckily, somebody has already written a "DiskEject" XCMD, so all you have to do is install the XCMD (using *ResEdit)*, and presto! HyperTalk now has a new command called "DiskEject." It works exactly like all the built-in commands; you can't tell the difference between an XCMD and an "original equipment" HyperTalk command. Technically, an XCMD is a small program written in a language like *C* or *Pascal*, compiled as a *resource* of type 'XCMD' and installed into a *stack*.

Xerox PARC (ZER ox PARK) Xerox Palo Alto Research Center. It was here, in the middle seventies, that the basis of the Mac *user interface* was created. Things we take for granted—icons, mice, windows, *bitmapped* fonts, and graphics on a *WYSIWYG* display—were all created here, as were laser printers, *Ethernet,* the *PostScript* language, and the *object-oriented* languages on which *HyperTalk* was later based. Quite a roster of achievements! What's even more remarkable is that although Xerox paid for all these breakthroughs, it never seriously tried to market any of them, and was left completely out in the cold when the personal computer revolution occurred. In the end, it was Apple (fertilized by PARC alumni) that brought the PARC innovations to the public in the form of the *Lisa* and the Mac.

The PARC researchers, led by Alan Kay and Adele Goldberg, had a far-reaching vision of the future of computing. At the time, using a computer meant either submitting decks of punch cards for *batch processing* or (if you were lucky) banging away on a mechanical Teletype terminal connected to a roomful of *mainframes* somewhere. But the PARC team foresaw a day when tremendous processor power would reside in an inexpensive, notebook-sized device they dubbed the "Dynabook." Writing in 1975, they described their vision thus: "We envision a device as small and portable as possible which could both take in and give out information in quantities approaching that of human sensory systems. Visual output should be, at the least, of higher quality than what can be obtained from newsprint. Audio output should adhere to…high fidelity standards. If such a machine can be designed in [such] a way that any owner can mold and channel its power to his own needs, then a new kind of medium will have been created."

That last sentence held the key to the PARC researchers' approach. Goldberg and Kay had faith that the technology would make the Dynabook's hardware feasible. The challenge as they saw it was to harness that power and make it serve the needs of everyone—not just computer science majors. "The hardware will come sooner or later, so we'd best get cracking on the software" was their unwritten motto. How well they succeeded we can see every time we look at a Mac—or a *PC* running *Windows*, or a *NeXT* machine—all of which embody interface concepts directly descended from the work done at PARC almost twenty years ago.

XFCN (EX FUNCTION) An "external" function added to *HyperCard;* once installed, it works just like a built-in *HyperTalk* function. Creating an XFCN is like creating an *XCMD*—write a program in *C* or *Pascal,* compile it as a *resource* of type 'XFCN,' and install it into your HyperCard *stack* with *ResEdit.* See the XCMD definition for more details.

x height The height of a lowercase letter "x"—hence, the average height (not counting *ascenders)* of most lowercase letters in a typeface. Studies have shown that a relatively large x height makes type more readable.

‡xylum

XMODEM (EX MOE DEM) A way of sending files from one computer to another, while checking to ensure that no errors occurred in transmission (due to noisy phone lines, for example). Devised by Ward Christensen in the mid-seventies, it has become a widely used standard.

There are several variants of XMODEM, and it's important to make sure that you're using the same version as the computer you're talking to before you try to transfer any files. The most common versions are standard XMODEM and CRC (Cyclic Redundancy Check) XMODEM, which provides slightly better error checking.

XPress (EX PRESS) Shorthand for Quark XPress, a large, powerful page layout program. Chronically plagued by bugs, it's often cynically referred to as "Quirk XPress" by its users—but for sheer power and features it's unequalled, and it has surpassed its chief rival, PageMaker, in sales.

XTND (EX TEND) A software technology developed by *Claris* that makes it possible to have a set of file-format translators that work with many different programs. For example, if you have an XTND translator for WordPerfect/Mac files, any program compatible with the XTND technology can use that translator to open WordPerfect files without needing to have its own knowledge of what they look like internally. It's a simple, efficient, modular way of doing things.

X

Yy

YARC (YARK) Yet Another Ruddy Coprocessor. A very fast, specialized *coprocessor* board for *NuBus* Macs like the IIci. The YARC board uses a *RISC microprocessor* that runs many times faster that the Mac's normal processor. The catch is that its AMD 29000 microprocessor is incompatible with standard Mac software, which needs Motorola's 68000 series *chips*. This means that only programs especially written for the YARC board—mostly graphics-oriented applications—will work with it. But for people who need to do very complicated graphics (such as image processing or 3D modeling) and can use one of the handful of YARC-compatible applications to do it, this board can save enormous amounts of time.

YMODEM batch (WYE MOE DEM BATCH) A variant of the *XMODEM* file transfer protocol, YMODEM uses 1K data blocks (for increased speed) and lets you specify a group of files to be sent as a batch. Could we have that in English, please? All right—it's a way of sending a bunch of files from one computer to another over the phone, using a *modem*. Okay? Boy, this telecommunications jargon gets pretty thick sometimes.

YMODEM G (WYE MOE DEM GEE) Yet another way of transferring files over the phone via *modem*. This one differs from its relatives *XMODEM* and *ZMODEM* in one important way: YMODEM G doesn't do any software error correction to make up for bad phone connections. It's meant to be used only with modems that have built-in error correcting hardware, as some newer, more expensive ones do. Because it doesn't need to waste time checking for errors, YMODEM G is faster than XMODEM.

Y

Zz

zap PRAM (ZAP PEE RAM) Reset-
ting the parameter RAM *(PRAM)* to
its *default* state. PRAM is a small
area of memory that's kept alive by
batteries, even when the Mac is
unplugged. This memory holds
things like the date and time, speaker volume, and which
drive is the startup disk. If your batteries die (common with
older Macs like the Plus), the contents of PRAM are lost
and you may have trouble printing or getting a hard disk
to be recognized. In that case, you need to "zap" your
PRAM to get it back to normal values.

To do this if you're running System 7, restart your Mac
while holding down the Command, Option, "P," and "R"
keys. You'll hear a second startup beep, then your Mac
will start up as usual. If you're using an earlier system (like
6.0.7), hold down the Command and Option keys while
pulling down the Apple menu and choosing "Control
Panel." You'll get a message warning you that you are
about to zap your PRAM. Go ahead and click "OK"—you
can't do any harm, and it may cure your problem.

ZMODEM (ZEE MOE DEM) The most advanced member
of the *XMODEM/YMODEM* family of file transfer protocols (ways of sending files from one computer to another
over the phone). ZMODEM has one important feature
that the others lack: it can resume an interrupted file
transfer. Let's say you're *downloading* a large graphics file
from a *BBS*. You've been on the phone for forty minutes
when suddenly a burst of static interrupts the transmission and the other computer hangs up on you. If you're
using ZMODEM, you can call back and resume downloading where you left off. With any of the other protocols,
you'd have to start over from the beginning, and your forty
minutes would have been wasted. Most Mac *telecommunications* programs now support the ZMODEM protocol.

Z

zone A group of *networked* computers, linked to other such groups by a *router* or *bridge*. Imagine, for example, that you want to wire your corporate headquarters for AppleTalk. You could put all 642 employees on the same network—but that would mean scrolling through a mighty long list whenever you wanted to send mail! Worse, that many people all trying to use the same network would lead to a tremendous traffic jam. The network would begin to make molasses in January look speedy by comparison.

Instead, you break the company's network into zones, each one a mini-network of its own: Engineering, Marketing, Production, Accounting, Research, Human Resources.

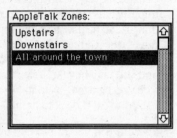

Users in each zone will be sending messages mostly to each other, but can talk to users in other zones anytime they want simply by selecting the desired zone in the *Chooser*. Because each zone carries only local traffic, the network doesn't bog down with too many users at once.

zoom box The small square area in the upper right corner of most Mac windows that lets you zoom the window up to fill the screen and then zoom it back to its original size. In System 7, the zoom box zooms *Finder* windows just large enough so that you can see all of their contents.

Say What?!

Alphabet Soup

AFP
AOL
ASCII
ATM
AU/X
BBS
BTW
C
CCITT
cdev
clut
CRT
DAL
DAT
DEC
DES
DIN
DOS
DXF

ELF
FKEY
FLA
fx
GIGO
GUI
HEPP
HFS
Hz
IAC
kbps
KISS
LC
LOL

lpi
MIPS
MUG
OCE
OOP
RTFM
SQL
SYLK
VAR
WDEF
WYSIWYG
YARC

Buzzwords

bundled
compatible
desktop
footprint
insanely great
look and feel
multimedia
object-oriented
OOP
Pink

plug and play
power user
real soon now
System 7 savvy
turbo
QuickTime
virtual reality
WYSIWYG

Graphics

clut
Gouraud shading
IGES
image processing
jaggies
JPEG
line art
lossy
palette
Pantone
PCX
Phong shading
PICT
PostScript
QuickDraw
radiosity

ray-tracing
RenderMan
RGB
TIFF
vector graphics
Wacom tablet